Witchcraft, Magic and Divination:
Accounts from the Wimbum Area of the Cameroon Grassfields

Patrick Mbunwe Samba

Langaa Research & Publishing CIG
Mankon, Bamenda

Publisher

Langaa RPCIG
Langaa Research & Publishing Common Initiative Group
P.O. Box 902 Mankon
Bamenda
North West Region
Cameroon
Langaagrp@gmail.com
www.langaa-rpcig.net

Distributed in and outside N. America by African Books Collective
orders@africanbookscollective.com
www.africanbookcollective.com

ISBN:9956-727-31-8

DISCLAIMER
All views expressed in this publication are those of the author and do
not necessarily reflect the views of Langaa RPCIG.

Table of Contents

Acknowledgments

I would like to thank the following people whose invaluable contributions enabled me to write this book.

Mrs. E. M. Chilver of Oxford University who urged me on several occasions to write a "true account" of the witchcraft in Binshua Village, North West Region, Cameroon. It was because of her insistence, the several letters she wrote, the questions and the comparative material she sent to me when I began writing that encouraged me to continue the venture. She did the final copy-editing and improved the layout and I must say that it was because of this support that I was determined to finish this work. To her, I am sincerely indebted;

Dr. Michael Rowlands of University College, London, who discussed aspects of his work when I began the writing and whose incisive comments on the topic gave me the insights to include the section 'Witchcraft and Religion' in this work;

Justice A. N. Njamsi of the Court of Appeal, Bamenda, whose very valuable comments on the section 'Witchcraft and the Law' moderated my very strong comments on this matter;

The Revd Dr. Englbert Kofon, Rector of the St. Thomas Aquinas Major Seminary Bambui, for the reading through the section. 3, and for his useful suggestions;

The Revd Father Chrysanthus Tim of Fundong Parish, whose enlightening replies to my queries about the Christian Church's stand on Witchcraft, helped to shape this section of the book;

Dr Omer Weyi Yembe whose encouraging analysis of the first part gave me the motivation to continue the exploration;

Mrs. Norma Ndoping for editing the manuscripts and making useful suggestions;

Dr. Loreto Todd of Leeds University for her encouragement and her early insistence that I should write something because anything written no matter how bad is better than nothing at all;

Papa Stephen Ndi of Cow Street Nkwen, who has continuously drummed into me that unless I write something and leave for prosperity he would consider me as having wasted my life;

Dr. Elizabeth Cockburn of Guelph University for her encouragement and support for the creative adventures both of us have undertaken since 1982;

Christopher Bobga formerly of ACT Office who typed the preliminary drafts in the early stages;

Above all, I am sincerely thankful for the financial support in the publication of this book provided by the African Studies Centre, University of Leiden in the Netherlands. I must pay tribute particularly to Professor Peter Geschiere of that Department whose initiative, because of his interest in this subject, enabled the Department to sponsor this publication and I think that his efforts will bear more fruits in the future.

And to all other friends who helped me in one way or the other I give my collective thanks. I do however, alone bear full responsibility for my errors, and would like to apologise in advance if this work inadvertently displeases anyone.

Patrick Mbunwe Samba
Bamenda

Preface

This is a personal testimony about witchcraft, magic and divination by someone who was born and bred in the area inhabited by the Wimbum tribe of the Republic of Cameroon, a country situated in the 'hinge' between West and Central Africa. Binshua, the village of my birth, is near Nkambe, the headquarters of Donga-Mantung Division in the North West Region of the Republic. I believe that the situation I describe, in which belief in witchcraft is all-pervading, can be found throughout Africa and in many other parts of the Third World, and is of great significance in so far as development is concerned. My aim in undertaking this research is to show how, by giving way to hysteria about an evil they do not understand, people perpetuate the evil through their own actions, thus becoming prisoners of their own obsession.

The first part of this account examines in depth, how, in a typical rural community, efforts to 'stabilise' the society operate in practice to the benefit of those who claim to know what to do and how to do it. It investigates the varying systems of divination and sorcery, describes witchcraft trials, and gives an account of the measures taken by medicine-men against witchcraft, as well as of other methods of combating witchcraft. It ends with the testimonies of others in section 2, which reveal the inhumanity of man to man manifested in manipulation of a community in which people allow themselves to be led into believing that disaster caused by witchcraft is constantly hovering over them.

In examining 'Witchcraft and The Law' in the third section, we discover how superficial, vague and ambiguous the law pertaining to matters of witchcraft is. Regrettably and after so many years of independence, we in Africa still show downright naivety and complacency in a matter of such of such significance to us, either owing to desire to cling to the vestiges of a cherished colonial upbringing or for the sake of a token recognition in international organisations irrespective of the realities we are facing in our daily lives in our village homes.

In the last section, 'Witchcraft and Religion', we reflect on the fact that practice of witchcraft is as old as man himself and is not a cancer particular to poor Africa, but an evil which the Christian Church has battled against over the centuries, all over the world.

It is suggested that the Church needs to do much more to free people from the fear of witchcraft, in which so many are still held. With the courage she has on account of her conscience, the Church is well suited to this task, and in carrying it out she will lead the way to free the downtrodden from poverty, disease and ignorance in which, in some cases, and in some countries, they are deliberately maintained by their oppressors.

Finally we look at modern forms of witchcraft, showing how rapidly belief in them is spreading.

In the Wimbum context in particular, and in Cameroon generally, witchcraft is not the preserve of one sex – both men and women are believed to practice it. In these accounts wherever the words witch, wizard or sorcerer are used it should be understood that we are referring to both sexes unless it is specifically stated otherwise.

The first part of the work consists largely of personal narrative and first hand description, and though accurate in fact is not presented as an anthropological paper. It is my sincere hope that this descriptive section will attract wide attention and provoke the thought of many, not just the experts in this field. It is also my belief that this matter should be one for general concern.

If after reading this work you are affected strongly enough to act or to change your attitude, or even if you simply enjoyed reading it, I shall be satisfied that the exercise has been a worthwhile endeavour.

Witchcraft, Magic and Divination
A Personal Testimony

Introduction

At the Binshua Village Development Association meeting of
August 23, 1984, I was personally accused of promoting and
encouraging the continuation of witchcraft in the village. The
reason for this pronouncement, from the more than 300
villagers who attended this development meeting, was that I
had defined witchcraft beliefs as the 'consequence of poverty,
disease, illiteracy and ignorance'. My intervention was
prompted by the work of sub-committee on witchcraft
practices which stated emphatically that Binshua Village was
full of witches who caused many of the deaths, particularly
among children, that take place in this village. It was for fear
of the action of the numerous witches, it was said that many
of the Binshua elite working out of the village refused to
come home.

The subcommittee on witchcraft practices, unlike other
committees had worked all day to try to come up with some
strongly-worded resolution on this theme. Thus my remark
was looked upon as an attempt to destroy the work that the
subcommittee had laboured at so hard, over a whole day, to
produce. 'Your tackles swords', said the spokesman, 'are
meant to give the witches solace and encouragement to
continue their nocturnal activities with fury. If we condemn
them in as many string words as we have done', the

spokesman continued, 'the witches will either fear to act indiscriminately, or they do not exist, you give them strength and support to act in that guise. Their numbers and activities are increasing these days because of the support they receive from increasing these days because of the support they receive from people like you. The instant deafening and hilarious applause the speaker received immediately convinced me that I might have made a mistake.

Of the more than 300 participants in the meeting, I was the only one who did not believe in witchcraft. The criticism against me was so strong that it only just fell short of naming me as one of the witches. It was a very acrimonious plenary session and the very tough resolutions taken at the meeting were testimony enough of the strength and depth of the feelings of the participants on this subject.

This was not the first time that I had stood up to put forward the idea of the non-existence of witchcraft of the type that the Binshua people believe in which some people 'eat' others mysteriously. Belief in this type of witchcraft has led to many hundreds of people being accused of it and exiled from the village, and has also forced many of the well-educated to escape from the village for fear that this or that uncle or aunt will 'eat' them. I had had opportunities to talk to people in 'Njanggi' (circulating credit clubs), drinking places, social groups and cooperatives, explaining that if such type of witchcraft really did exist very few people would still be extant in this wicked world. I had pointed out that God could not have given that type of power to anybody and that if anyone believed in God truly, even if he were not a Christian, and more so was bold and fearless then that nothing would affect that person.

Many people would listen attentively and ask questions, but would believe me only for as long as they and the members of their family were not afflicted by sickness. It is difficult to convince people, who have been brought up to believe so, that sickness is not caused by witchcraft, some terribly cruel and some frightening. I have been an eye-witness of numerous witchcraft judgements, deaths and exiles; I have seen the complete abandonment of entire compounds, and the terrible agony of mind caused to men and women, in particular to those accused of eating this or that relative, and heartlessly 'given a bamboo' with an order to leave the village for good.

What is more disturbing is the fact that in spite of the impact of education, and the level of political and economic awareness of the population of the village, and in spite of the increasing influence of Christianity and the nearness to the administrative authority, the belief in the existence of witchcraft not only persists, but also controls the lives of so many of my people. The pity of it all is that it saps their ability to adapt traditionally to the rapid social changes they are experiencing and to make the choices with which they are comforted.

The role of the Chief

Binshua village (population c.6030) is four kilometres from Nkambe Town, the capital of the North West Province of the Republic of Cameroon. It is not a remote village but lies on the Bamenda-Nkambe section of the Ring Road, which connects many of the Province's administrative centres. It has remained famed for the strong stance it takes against the slightest suspicion of witchcraft. The village chief-a very dynamic 51 year old ex-forestry labour foreman takes immediate action to punish severely in order to deter completely. His fame in dealing with such matters is known beyond the village and many people praise him saying 'This is how a Chief should rule'. He is in complete control of all his people'. If this is true of the present Chief, it is truer still of his predecessor, his late father. Given their viewpoint, many people look on Binshua with envy, and neighbouring chiefdoms are known to consult the Chief of Binshua from time to time. The Chief, like many others of his rank, is believed to see what is coming and he usually warns his village folk that there is an impending danger, such as death in a particular family, or a famine or an epidemic. Yet death continues to visit the village and so the Chief continues to punish. Tradition imposes on a Chief certain obligations, as well as rights and rites, which cannot be questioned by mortal men. At least I have never witnessed sum an affront during my growing-up in this village; any criticism would be taken as such. Nevertheless, I believe that some reflection and reassessment is necessary in this day and age.

From time to time the Chief invites his sub-chiefs, quarter and ward heads to the palace to alert them that he 'saw' a coffin coming from outside to the village. That night a 'juju' – a secret society member in a net face-covering, from the palace – goes out to announce that the people who are trying to bring about that event should desist from attempting it, because they have been detected. The elders from the particular compound are warned to halt the action of witchcraft, and should they be in doubt as to its source they go out to consult a diviner, known in Cameroon English as a 'nggambe man' or in Limbum as a nwe seng (plural = *ngaa seng*), who is expected to reveal what is happening. Meanwhile

4

the maternal uncles of the supposed victim then consult another *nwe seng*, a reputable one outside the neighbourhood. These maternal uncles usually arrive at the compound where the death of their nephew is expected, before dawn, to show their extreme concern. All the people come out to the courtyard to hear their message, which is usually delivered by their spokesman.

The message might include an accusation of a person in that compound, in which case he or she would be exiled, or it could direct that attention be paid to some ancestor. Whichever is the case, in order to stop the impending danger, goats, fowls and other things are taken to the Chief, who pronounces the sentence of exile if a living person is the source of danger, or directs that a sacrifice be done if the problem can be solved by appeasing an ancestor. This process of consultation, i.e. the checking with various ngaa seng, operates only when there is an impending danger. In the event of a sudden death the chief usually acts immediately and decisively, according to the circumstances.

In order to stop witches escaping from the village, and to bar others from entering it, the Chief sometimes sends the important elders to symbolically protect the realm and to seal off all entrances into the village. At each entrance therefore the priests in charge of this ritual place a small gourd with "powerful" medicine in it, and cross the calabashes with two *nwaa* (a green plant resembling a *Ialang grass*). They split open the beak of a fowl, and the gushing blood is allowed to collect into the pot. When the ritual is finished any witch who tries to re-enter, or who wants to leave, is supposedly caught in the vessel. It is said that if you see any living thing in that pot, for example a fly or an ant, it is somebody who has been 'caught', and that he or she would die. It is stated, however, that

5

powerful witches sometimes find alternative entrances. In many villages in the Wimbum area a powerful juju called *Soo'*, which women are not allowed to see, sometimes walks round all the boundaries of the village and seals them off. In addition, charms or fetishes are hung above the roads at junctions leading into the village in order to keep off flying witches. Sometimes, of course, the prediction of the Binshua Chief comes true, and this may happen to such an extent that even a non-believer in the art of seer ship cannot ignore the coincidence without attracting public ridicule. For example, it was said at one time that a worker would die in Ntungap Quarter in Papa Samba's fiuni1y in less than a month if the elders did not avert the situation. The elders were asked as usual to 'arrange their house' quickly. They appeared to have taken some action but ... After three weeks Mr. Atbanasius Samba, a civil servant from Binshua working in Binju, died, it was said, as the result of his coming into contact with a mysterious substance while he was cleaning his yard. A medical autopsy stated tetanus to be the cause of his sudden death.

The sudden and tragic death of this important member of the *elite* of Binsbua Village, which death the Chief had predicted, shook the villagers, as well as the Chief and his councillors. The news of this dramatic event went round in the manner of dry season bush-fire and caught people like an electric shock. Reflecting on my experience of village life generally, and of incidents like this one in particular, I expected a terrible reaction to result from this death and I regretted inwardly that this episode should happen while I was around again. However, Providence would come to our aid, I hoped.

This death happened to take place on 21 August, 1984, just two days before a meeting of the Binshua Village Development Association was scheduled – the meeting of which I referred to in my introduction. The meeting had been p1amed a year in advance and many delegates had a1ready began to arrive from various parts of the country, so as to prepare for this very important event. The consensus among many villagers, which was also rapidly gaining easy acceptance among some of the delegates from outside of the Division, was that, in honour of and out of respect for the late Athanasius Samba, the meeting should be postponed. I did not hesitate to point out very forcefully that, however important this death was, it would be illogical to plan a meeting a year in advance and suddenly cancel it at the last minute, solely because of the death of one of us. At :first my views sounded strange and unorthodox, but our contribution to the organization of the burial ceremonies, to the entertainment of the visitors and mourners, the way we served rather than seeking to be served, and in general the way and manner in which the Binshua *elite* from outside of the village handled the entire death celebration, impressed everyone. This was because this was the first occasion of this type in the village where *elites* from outside were servants to the ordinary people rather than masters. I had advised that none of us should eat or drink until the visitors and villagers bad been properly attended to. Our financial contribution too was very significant, and I even ended up contributing far more than I had pledged because I found myself having to settle some of the unpaid bills some days later! Everything went very smoothly and our meeting was held on schedule although, surprisingly, the village Chief did not show up, and neither did a few of the *elite* noted for having views like the Chief's.

Meanwhile, when all these activities were taking place an astonishing thing was going on among the late Athanasius' family members and among the people of the entire Ntungap Quarter which, as far as the rest of us were concerned, came to light only six months later.

Bimhua Catholic Mission is the oldest Mission outstation of Nkambe Parish. A Reverend Father from Nkambe main mission used to offer Holy Mass every Sunday to the very devoted and enthusiastic Christians there. Some weeks after the death celebration of the late Athanasius Samba Ngiri, however, the Reverend Father did not appear for the usual Sunday mass. Christians thought of possible reasons for that unusual happening, but when the following week and the next came and passed without the Reverend Father appealing, there was bewilderment, even agitation. The very ardent Christians, who were hungrier than most for Christ, took off for the Parish headquarters to unravel the mystery behind this strange behaviour of the man of God.

Meanwhile rumours had been circulating about an extraordinary happening at the Ntungap Quarter during the death celebration of the late Athanasius. The rumour source was traced to the Catechist of Binshua, who had probably hinted to the Reverend Father what the goings-on were during those agonizing times in Ntungap.

It was said that in order to put a final stop to the type of witchcraft practice which took away important people like the late Athanasius Samba from the village, the entire people of Ntungap Quarter took a solemn oath that· such a death would never occur in Ntungap Quarter again. In order to seal the secret oath, as ordained by the tradition of their ancestors, they slaughtered a dog and mixed the blood with a concoction of traditional medicines, and everyone went through the ordeal of licking the mixture as a sign that they would give up the practice of witchcraft.

It is to this story that the man of God was reacting, so indicating that he considered the Binshua people to be pagans.

For several months the people were starved of the Body of Christ and the story preached about in churches – and what wonderful sermons they were! Negotiations went on for a good many months until finally the people submitted to a very severe punishment to atone for their sins, and later went to Confession. Afterwards the man of God resumed his visits to Binshua.

In their hearts of hearts the members of the Binshua family concerned believed that they had benefited doubly – they had cleared their way with their God as well as 'arranged their house' traditionally with their ancestors. Whether they were right or wrong is a matter we cannot debate now. It is safer: to await another test of will when a similar tragedy occurs in this Quarter or elsewhere in Binshua. Only then can we begin to know what is what.

In the neighbouring town of Nkambe there was another incident: it was announced that someone would die at the market and that the man concerned would be a stranger. A week later a foreigner was killed in an accident at the market in circumstances which were difficult to unravel. Ritual cleansing was held to be necessary before the market could go into operation again.

In the very recent past some of the elders of the nearby Binju village boasted that they were responsible for bringing the Government Station to Binju In filet, the Government

Station was actually built there shortly after a smallpox epidemic had caused the death of almost the entire population of this village, whereas other villages close by were not affected. Forty-one years after these incidents, these revelations concerning the creation of the Government Station in Binju and its supposed relationship with the smallpox epidemic brought by these men, some of whom are living today, still baffle many people. I shall treat the concept involved, called *nje nchang* by the Wimbum, in the next section.

However; the predictors are not always so lucky. The Chief predicted that a coffin of an educated man working out of the village was to be brought to our compound. The person named as about to die, who was in good health, lived in Douala. Nearly five years later nothing has happened. But I know full well that if anything should happen to him, even today, many will still believe that it is in fulfilment of that old prediction. When I asked my uncles and other older relatives why there was no panic on their part and why they did not hurry to act on what the Chief had foretold, they told me that Boonko family bad renounced witchcraft a long time ago. They have a shrine at a location called Mbinko where their forefathers and they themselves took an oath never to get involved in witchcraft. They drank *nggur* (sasswood) as a sign of that bond, and thus no person from Boonko has ever joined witch groups. It was believed that any individual who 'went out' would himself automatically die without any other family member being affected. That is why, they have said, that whenever witch groups were passing at night, the people in Boonko (who do claim to 'see' would raise their hands up showing that they have nothing to do with them. 'That is why', they went on, 'we do not have unusual or suspicious:

deaths in Boonko, and that is why,' they concluded, 'all of our' children are so progressive'. It was also revealed to me that once in a while the elders would make a pilgrimage to *Mbinko*, the secret shrine of the Boonko family, to offer sacrifices, to perform a neglected ritual or to pour a libation to our ancestors. Thus, whatever the Chief or any person may predict about any person from the Boonko family, is not taken seriously, and there are very few instances in which a member of our family went to consult a *nwe seng*, a 'nggambe man'.

Types of Witchcraft beliefs

Many of the witchcraft accusations in Binshua Village and in many villages in the Wimbum area concern the mystical 'eating' of people, the activity of the a *tfu yingwe* – cannibal witches. Whenever somebody died in a family, a relative suspected of being a witch is accused of having given him to repay a debt of someone else's flesh he bad supposedly eaten. It is only a near relative who can hand over a person to pay a debt to his witchcraft group. Sometimes, given timely intervention, a future victim can be saved if the giver reveals the secret of the deal in time. This often happens, particularly when the accused person's witch partners are alleged to have demanded a much more important person from his family than they themselves had in turn provided from theirs. If this happens, and it is common knowledge, the rescue operation will be performed by a traditional priest who will demand a series of .things for sacrifice. If this is not done and the accused person refuses to fulfil his bargain with his witch partners, he may be expected to die through their power.

11

Very often an elder in the village is accused of "opening the eyes" of some young persons so as to enable them to become witches, by giving them *nya nwe*, the flesh of a human being, which is always dried. In the many instances I heard of when I was growing up, it is the children who report that when they were going to fetch water this or that elder called them to give them meat. The late Ta Tumanta Kobo, an uncle, was accused by many children in our compound of doing this. These beliefs very common in Binshua Village, and even the former Catechist of tile Catholic Church in Binshua was accused of giving human meat to some children. In such cases people come out in the morning and the children are given fowls with which to hit the accused person in broad daylight. After the child bas hit the suspected person the fowl is supposed to die immediately to show it has been accepted in lieu of the child. The act is held to end the mater. If the fowl does not immediately this indicates that the lad will still be pursued, in which Case the elders take some other action.

In a very recent case I heard of in Taku village, one of the Chief's wives was accused and hit with two fowls. One of the fowls died and the other did not. A man from a neighbouring village came by at that very moment and touched the dead fowl with a walking stick, asking whether the chicken was really dead, which would imply that the *wiinto* or chief's wife, was guilty. Immediately the chicken came back to life. This caused an additional crisis. If was then alleged that the man was a member of the woman's witch group and had come to encourage the woman not to allow herself to be bit with the fowls, so that the group would get its victim. This situation is currently being handled by the elders.

It is certainly odd that the "dried flesh" of some important people, who died nearly 30 years ago, is said to be still being carried about in Binshua. If you were to ask many people in Binshua about that today, they are certain to tell you that the flesh of a famous politician from Tabenken, the late J. T. Ndze, and that of the late Gabriel Nfor, a police officer from Binshua, is 'still being carried about by witches in the Wimbum area today. Since these people were important, it follows that those witches who supposedly took part in 'eating' them have to 'give' people of equal standing. Many Binshua people pointed to an avocado pear tree at the entrance to the Catholic Mission yard from the Mula road as the place where the witches had stored the dry meat in a'*nkeng*,' a raffia basket.

Five years ago the stories about the avocado pear tree and the dried human meat bad grown to such wild proportions that the pear tree was cut down. Since then witchcraft fears have grown worse and the Chief now finds it difficult to handle them alone. A group of middle-aged men from all over the village has recently decided to deal with witches by forming themselves into a dancing group called *atara*. Their main aim is to show any suspected witch that the village as a whole will not give them permission to act. It is too early to estimate their impact yet. .

Tfu yingwe, witchcraft for eating people, is the most feared witchcraft. The witches are, as a rule, regarded as acting in groups either at village or even at clan level. The witches cannot 'eat' a person who has not been 'given' to them (by a relative) in repayment of a debt by that relative who, in principle, is a member of the group. The group is always said to include a woman. Quite often she is the one without mercy and is usually the one who mystically gives the victim a mortal

13

blow with a club. We are informed that some witches 'give' relatives to that society simply out of jealousy and malevolence; some are motivated, rather, by the desire to inherited property, and others do it because they joined the society unknowingly and have to abide by its rules, since they believe that they themselves will die if they do not fulfil their own part of the deal.

It is believed in Binshua that everybody is potentially a witch but that the practice is not developed in every person. It is' said that each person has witch knowledge in his or her "stomach", but that this has to be turned upside down if he or she is to be capable of 'seeing'. That is why young people whose witchcraft potentials are to be realized are supposed to be initiated by being held up by their legs with their heads pointing downwards.

One of the most popular stories about witchcraft practice in the Wunbum area concerns an imaginary land or realm called *nje nchang*, which is where witches go to attend market. *Nje nchang* may be described as the witch market. There is one place recognized as such in the Wunbum area. It is the highest point in the area between Binka and Mfumnte, called Mbintong, a plateau full of *mye'* or white stones. It is generally believed that one can' only go to this place thrice in his or her life.

In order to be able to travel to *nji nchang* witches are expected first of all to be transformed into animals, to bring back things which may turn out to be good or bad. It is said that people have 'gone for *psa*.' People who are supposed to have been there are believed to have brought back such things as wealth, fertility in both men and animals, an abundant yield of food crops, a good singing voice, or new dances. It is believed to be especially lucky to go to *nje chang* in

14

the company of a Chief. This fact is alleged to lead to the curing of a chronic disease. Conversely, one could also bring back a disease, ill-luck, a windborne plague or some other dangerous things. It is also possible to come back with nothing at all, and people who do not have 'four eyes' would not even see anything during their visit to *nje nchang*.

It is said that the king of the place, who is called *nkfu nchang*, and his wife, called *ngwa nchang*, or *maa nchong*" together with all their subjects, are thoroughly evil. It is generally believed that when the market in *nje nchang* is in full session, the *nkfu nchang* begins an extremely interesting dance so that the foolish ones among the visitors spend their time watching it. During this time, he sends his people to lay a very slippery liquid substance on the road out of there so that when they start chasing the visitors, the later would slip and fall and it then becomes easy to catch them. If one's spirit-double is caught he/she then begins to grow thin and eventually the actual body dies. But the clever visitors it is alleged, Usually are not expected to allow themselves to be deceived by the diversionary tactics of the *nkfu nchang*. It is said, in witchcraft legends that as soon as these clever ones have picked up their parcels, which are tied up in leaves, they depart in a hurry to cross the big stream which marks the boundary of *nje nchang* and the physical world. When they are safe on the other bank, each one opens up his leaf-parcel. Those who discover that they have picked plagues or ill-luck may throw the parcels into the river and hurry home. They are supposed to have been unfortunate on this terribly dangerous trip. Those who happen to pick up good fortune carry it home and in some situations the entire chiefdom benefits. It is also said that some wicked people who discover that they have picked up say, smallpox or a locust plague, or poverty, maliciously bring

15

this to the village and innocent people then suffer from the malediction until many sacrifices have been performed and the witches are found out and exiled. The smallpox which killed off almost all of the population of Binju Village prior to the location of the Division Headquarter there in 1947 is said to have been brought about by some wicked people who had picked it up from *nje nchang*. Some Binju people say that the use of smallpox was the sacrifice to facilitate the bringing of the Divisional Headquarters to their village. In the Wunbum magico-religious belief these people are said to have *duu psa* that is, gone to the land of tempting wealth.

In Binshua, as well as in all the other villages of the Wunbum clan, it is believed, as already mentioned, that witches can transform into different animals. Snakes and birds are included. These animal doubles (e.g. leopard-doubles, monkey-doubles, owl-doubles, goat-doubles) are alleged to have the capacity to destroy crops or to destroy other animals, particularly domestic animals and even to kill human enemies. Some witches, however, change into snakes to do good; in Tabenken village, for example, one Papa Nformi Bambo of Tfum was reported to treat complex fractures with the assistance of a huge snake (python) which slip into the house after the patient had been warned not to panic. Upon entry into the house it would lick the area of the fracture, then wrap itself around the place thus arranging the pieces of bones back in place and disappearing after some minutes. My cousin was cured by the man in 1955 and thousands of people have received treatment from him. Except for this python-double treatment, the results of which I have seen myself: most transformations take place at night. In the Wimbum area we call people who transform *ngaa byer buu*. One needs particular leaves; which if eaten are capable of

16

transforming the eater into whatever creature the leaves could transform him/her into. Many witches are said to change from one state into another almost at will, but care has to be taken because it is said that if one were discovered in the process of transformation, one might remain halfway through it, thus eventually dying without having either fully 'recovered' or fully transformed.

There are other types of witchcraft beliefs in the Wimbum in which a kind of transformation is involved. One such type is described as *njirr*. A *njirr* is actually the ghost or image of a dead person. it is lifeless and its main occupation is to frighten people either in the farms, in a forest or on empty waste land with thickets.

It makes a noise, and people run away when they hear the voice of a *njirr*.

It is commonly believed in Binshua that when an important witch is to die people see his/her image elsewhere in the land; that is to say that, his ghost has come out of him and is leaving his village to go to another place. Whenever many people complain that a *njirr'* has frightened them the elders predict that an important man would die – and sometimes this actually happens. I have not heard of any occasion when a *njirr* is reported to have killed someone.

Very closely related to the *njirr* is a *nyurkaa*. A *nyurkaa'* is different from anji" in that it is the spirit of a living person – a spirit-double. The human person is still alive while his spirit moves around to frighten people. It supposedly takes pleasure in frightening people but, like a *njirr*, it is not connected with' eating' anybody. A nyurlcod is capable of increasing in height, particularly when it is chasing people. Stories of *njirr* and *nyurkaa'* have not been frequent in recent years, and some people attribute this to the growth in

17

population and to the effective occupation by men or cattle of the Binshua lands and the complete disappearance of the virgin forest in the chiefdom

There is another kind of witch belief in which the victim is convinced that he is being throttled at night. In Limbum we call it *tfu nyo' nwe*. Sometimes people dismiss this as a dream. But from the account of former victims of *tju nyo nwe* the phenomenon resembles the type of nightmare in which the victim is semi-conscious. On many occasions in Binshua, people have reported that they are being throttled every night. Some say that every night someone they know comes to throttled them while demanding the settlement of an outstanding' debt'. In this case, upon the victim's complaint the elders would call in the suspect and settle the matter. If the act is repeated after the judgment, sometimes a *nggambe man* is consulted and if the suspect is confirmed as guilty the same preventive measure are taken as in a case where someone is suspected of initiating people into witchcraft. Alternatively the suspect is exiled. Closely connected with stories of throttling people are the many stories and complaints by women of their being forced into sexual intercourse by invisible beings who come at night. In some recent cases, where the woman was pregnant, this sexual intercourse once or twice was held to make her miscarry. A relation of mine is facing this problem at this very moment, but I have not been able to find a cure as yet. If you can advise on this we will be very grateful.

Some people are also known to *fuutfu*, i.e. to bewitch themselves. It is said that some witches, if intensely offended by a rebuke from a member of the family for some wrongdoing, will 'bring out' (*fuutfu*) his or her witchcraft and die. If any person dies and then his corpse swells up, the

Binshua people do not bury him in the compound; but in the bush, and there is no mourning, because the belief is that if you send him to the next world with glory he will always return to bother the living. Many people *fuutfu*, 'bring out their witchcraft and die', because they are jealous of the things others have. An unsuccessful businessman, a man without a child, a very lazy fellow, will be jealous (*ko'ndong*) of a successful relative, and decide to *fuutfu* and die. Some suicides can be attributed to this. We call such people 'a person with a stomach', *nwe rbuur*; perhaps this is because witchcraft is supposed to reside in the stomach of its host.

A sort of witchcraft, sorcery rather, in the Wimbum area is connected with the sending of thunder and lightning. If someone takes your wife, or owes you a debt and stubbornly refuses to pay, you could consult a lightning sender (*nwe-tusi-sa "-mbeng*) to obtain vengeance. An important aspect here is that you must be sure of your claim that the person about to be attacked is really guilty; if lightning is sent to an innocent person it is alleged to come back to kill the complainant. There are many people in the Wimbum area who claim to have either sent or to have witnessed the sending of, or know people who send thunder and lightning to destroy property or to kill someone. It is claimed that this magical art can only be employed during the rainy season.

In the late 'fifties particularly, witchcraft-fears haunted many people in Binshua Village, to the extent that at night people would have all sorts of nightmares of witches. It was common, too, to see someone abandon a journey halfway and return home because he saw a chameleon on the road, or because an animal crossed the road from his left to his right, or he/she hit his right toe – all bad omens. It was also possible to see someone returning from a journey wailing because he saw a kite in the sky hovering in one place above him/her, seeming to dance, which signified that he/she would lose an important member of the family. It has been extremely difficult to convince my wife that if two cats caterwaul near our house an important member of the family will not die, because she will point to an incident four years ago when this happened. She recently informed me when my uncle died that the death was predicted because a plantain in our backyard which bad just formed fell off the stern, and someone had told her that it signified something bad. It was even worse when an owl hooted over our house at night or a cock crowed at midnight, because these are all supposed to be omens of evil. All these accidental, common place happenings and many other odd natural phenomena frighten many Binshua people badly, because anything unusual or adverse that happens is considered to be the action of a witch. To live and survive in this society, where every unexplained incident is beclouded with fear and suspicion, day in and day out, is an experience which most people would prefer to avoid. But in Binshua it is part of everyday life; only a casual visitor would feel embarrassed by the witchcraft scenarios I have described, which are taken as in the nature of things.

Divination and sorcery as counter-measures

Any society afflicted by a paranoia of this magnitude, that of considering witchcraft influences as governing all the facets of human life, or in which an infinite variety of events are ascribed to witchcraft, must look for counter-measures compatible with this closed system of belief The Wimbum in general and the Binshua man in particular is equal to this task.

As was stated earlier, whenever disaster strikes in the form of a death or sickness or lightning, witchcraft is suspected; the immediate reaction is to consult a *nwe seng*, or diviner, who would usually determine the cause, but does not necessarily prescribed a cure. If the death was of someone note-worthy, the agnatic family and the dead man's nephews (sisters' sons) go separately to consult different diviners to see if they can come up with a consensus as to the cause of the death. Various solutions are propounded. Very often an ancestor is said to be angry, or a ritual has been neglected, or someone owed him a grudge or a relative has 'given' him to repay a 'debt'.

There are many types of diviners in the Mbum area and all over the Division. A common type of divination consists of throwing a number of objects on the floor: the diviner then interprets the way they fall and the way the objects lie in relation to one another.

The first step is that you tell the diviner what the problem is, and he or she will then throw the objects on the floor and start to tell you where the problem has arisen or who is responsible for causing it and how you can arrive at solving it. Because many of the diviners or *ngaa-seng-seng* do not prescribe a cure, the victim or the people concerned go to some other people, called *ngaamchep*, whose job it is to solve the problem or seek revenge. In many cases people who consult a *nwe-seng* have already made up their minds who the person responsible for the trouble is, and if their view is not confirmed they move from one diviner to another. Usually diviners ask you leading questions to elicit: facts which they later use. Others do not ask you anything after you have made your initial introductory remarks to expose the problem. Sometimes diviners surprise people with startling facts which are found to be true in the end. Many are evidently quacks and charlatans, others astute psychologists.

Diviners have different objects with which they perform.

This range from a few simple cowry shells, the inner skin of cola nuts, pieces of leather and wild garden-eggs, to a large collection of different bones, pebbles and many oddments of assorted size, shape and colour. Paul Gebauer's book *Spider Divination* (Milwaukee, 1964) indicates the complexity of some of the diviners' stock-in-trade in some of the ethnic groups in this part of Donga-Mantung. The casting and reading of these objects is an art that is very fully developed in the Mbum area, and there are a number of general interpretations with which we will not concern ourselves here. Suffice it to say that some of these master craftsmen do manage to reduce, at least temporarily, the tensions which the victims of misfortune and their kinfolks are subjected to.

Although it is difficult to generalize beyond my own group, one could say that many people in Cameroon completely believe in witchcraft and take counter-measures have known many highly educated people who wear amulets and 'layas' for their' protection. I also know a good number of intellectuals and highly placed people who rush back to their village with their families for their parents to 'check their heads' because within one week they might have been involved in two car accidents, or the children are not doing well in school, or they have been constantly ill. I know a renowned politician who must spend nearly half of his quite substantial salary to maintain a number of' 'malabos' and medicine-men so as to be invulnerable to the many people he imagine would try to undermine him in all sorts of ways. He would tell you openly and candidly that he is 'invincibly the day he even told us that if anything happened in the room in

22

which we were drinking, let us say some "enemies" were to come to attack us, 'no one will see me because I will place my back against the wall and just disappear'. Many people believe his claims because he has remained a parliamentarian for very many years, despite the fact that people seeking emolumentary positions like his, desirable since there is much poverty in our society, would fight to unseat the incumbent by any means, including slander and threats. He told people recently that he has now acquired some 'terrible rings from India' and that any person standing election against him will die. However, we know that as society develops and as more people become enlightened, these tactics no longer convince many people.

Here is an example of the more lucrative aspects of divination. I know a recent case of a highly qualified lady school teacher who borrowed a large sum of money to give to a herbalist cum diviner in order to save her junior sister from the ' imminent death' which the medicine-man had predicted. This situation arose when there was a violent clash between the police and the population during which the younger brother of this lady was killed. She was directed to this famous medicine-man, who was reputed to recall the dead and get messages from them for surviving members of the family. When the lady got to the shrine her late brother was conjured up from the dead and one of the messages which he is said to have delivered was that if nothing serious was done to protect the rest of the family then they would all die. Realizing that she had lost her four-year old son in circumstances she could not explain on this same day the previous year, she was very frightened and indeed in a panic. She rushed back to the medicine man who started to perform miracles in order to rescue her sister, predicted by the

23

medicine-man to be the next victim. This innocent girl was studying and was in one of our secondary schools. When the teacher told me the situation I decided to stand in for her husband and to see these wonders for myself, hearing the voice of a dead person invoked by the medicine-man for example. This would be a useful experience for me, thought. When we got there we were taken to the sanctuary but instead of letting us see what the lady was promised if she brought the remaining money, the man suddenly became irritable and angry, and started asking why the lady bad ' brought me. Meanly just fell short of pushing me out of the sanctuary. I sat quietly and at ease and made no statement at all. Finally the man invited me to another room to show me an album and pictures of his children in the United States. 'This one here is doing medicine and this other one is doing engineering', he said. When I indicated that we were about to leave be went out to see me off, now treating me with a good deal of respect, although there were very many important and rich people from Santa, Bafoussam and Yaoundé there. I was not surprised at the reaction of the medicine-man. The lady teacher suggested that perhaps our 'eyes' did not agree. On our way back I told the lady that the fellow was a fraud. I regretted that she had wasted this advance of about £400 or' 200.000 francs CFA, which she had paid out of fear. I assured her that the gentleman, who is almost a millionaire now, was trading on the ignorance and gullibility of innocent folks and building a, huge fortune for bimself I preached to her throughout the journey but she said nothing, and in the next few days (I only learnt of this six months after) she sneaked back with the junior sister, finished paying the balance of about the same amount, and got her sister and others in the family 'protected' from the calamity she was made to believe was facing them. She would not take the risk of my being wrong in my diagnosis. This medicine-man may be a good herbalist but I don't believe he is a prophet!

This incident is fairly typical, not only of the villages, but also of the cities of our country, and Christians as well as pagans is involved.

Many people in Binshua who are victims of misfortune and who suspect that witchcraft is the cause go to *nkieng*; that is they go to a type of diviner-sorcerer who purports to kill the suspect by slaying him in a mysterious manner. The diviner brings a bowl of water and puts this on the floor. The client pronounces the name of the thief or suspected witch and the witch-finder calls up the person with a ritual invocation, and if the charge is true the image of this person supposedly appears in the water. Then, with sharp needles, the image is pierced by the consultant himself and the person is supposed to die either immediately or from gradual wasting away, leading to death shortly thereafter.

I witnessed two incidents of this nature when I was still young. In one instance, besides the many People holding sharp needles which they used in piercing the image in the water, there were many other people stationed at the four corners of the house and at road junctions and entrances, armed with cutlasses. As soon as the image appeared and the first person was about to pierce it with a needle, a signal was given and every person inside and outside followed him, either piercing with a needle or cutting the ground with cutlasses this way and that several times in simultaneous action, in case the witch was a very strong one and was attempting to escape. There was absolutely dead silence and tension during the period of waiting for the image to appear in the bowl of water. Sometimes the inquirer would not 'see' the particular person he thinks has killed his relative and will repeat the session. Only very serious cases are taken to *nkieng* diviners and few such people still exist in the Wimbum area today. There are still very famous ones in the Yamba area of Nwa Subdivision in Donga Mantung Division, to which some people from the Wimbum area still go, trekking for four days or more.

The Arts of Divination, Sorcery and Weather-magic recalled

In the late 'forties and early 'fifties, when I was growing up in the village, spider divination was a very common practice in Binshua Village. Besides the Chief of the village, whose fame had spread beyond it for his skill in this art, there were a few other people who were also to be reckoned with. But we were more in touch with what the Chief did at his spider sanctuary because he never went very far from the village fur the divination.

Whenever the Chief discovered an earth-spider hole anywhere near the village, he used to prepare the place by sweeping the front clean or levelling the ground properly, He then built a shelter over the hole and placed a number of small sticks in front of it. When the time for consultation came he recited his request and asked the spider to give an answer. He would then retire to the 'palace and return on the following morning. If the complaint was that someone was seriously ill, and the supplicant wanted to know what was wrong, and what could be done to save his or her life, and the spider was discovered to have brought out soil from the hole and dumped it by the mouth of the hole, that was supposed to, be the signal that the person would die. But if the sticks

26

were only disturbed or were scattered around the hole, the Chief would interpret the position of the sticks and determine the cause of tile sickness. He would then return to deliver his findings. As small children we used to sit around and watch the Chief return from divination place. Usually he would smile at us, in which case knew that all was well, but if be just passed us looking serious stem and walking fast, we knew, young as we were, that a terrible thing would occur yet again. We would then report to our parents when they returned in the evening, some saying: 'Mama, the Chief returned from the shrine looking stem and angry.' Usually that night, or on the following morning of such a day, there would be a message or a signal from the palace summoning the four quarters of Binshua to congregate and listen to some instructions or to hear a revelation. Life was not too happy in those days because almost every week we were led to expect that some disaster was hovering about us.

Some diviners use only the inner covering or pericarp of a cola nut seed. We call such diviners in Limbum, *ngaa njoo'*. When five slices of the inner covering of a cola nut seed are tossed onto the ground by a diviner (*nwe njoo'*) or by the supplicant, a good diviner can reveal many things about the person by the way the things fall and how they lie in relation to one another. On 21.4.88 as I was interviewing a Mbum lady of nearly 70 years of age about this phenomenon, she told me she was only just recovering from a sickness which she had been suffering from for the past six years. She confided to me that her sickness was predicted by a *nwe njoo'* before ever she fell sick, and that it had come to pass exactly as the man foretold. I did not question her about what she told me because her candour was very convincing.

There was another woman in the next apartment who was interested in our conversation. She cut in to tell me an interesting story about when she began giving birth to her male children. 'One day as I walked past a hut where people were drinking, a man offered me a bottle of palm wine. When it was opened it kept foaming, even when it was put in a tumbler. This kind gentleman asked me to sit down and then revealed to me that the baby that would come from the pregnancy I was carrying would be a boy. It came out truly that when I gave birth it was a boy, my first, and. since that time I have had only boys. It has been wonderful.' She informed me that from her experience whenever she was warned by somebody that this or that would happen, it always came to be so, and that if she were to take off for a journey and someone said that something adverse would happen she would not dare to move. There was no reason for me trying to find out more details, but I advised her to let me know about any such incidents in the future since she said it happens to her 'all the time'.

The other method of divination I know about was the type my father practiced. It is called in Limbum *kad* – the use of a wild garden egg for divination. The wild garden egg is broken into five parts. After the top of the fruits chopped off and discarded the *nggor*, or stem, is removed and the rest of the fruit cut into four equal parts. This is all that was used by my father to baffle many people with.

My father was a strong '*nggambe* man' (*nwe seng*). His art was very simple but very profound, and in so far as "*kad*" was concerned his fame was uncontested. I used to carry his bag on treks to far off villages, where many people consulted him on various problems of the family and the village. The locality in which he usually operated was the area to the north of

Binshua Village, particularly the villages of Bih, Sab, Mbaanjeng, and Bomansuh. Sometimes he went as far afield as Mbipye. Sometimes he was invited to visit, but otherwise we made a tour of this area routinely about twice a month.

It is quite possible that if schooling had not diverted me I would have become a very strong *kaa* diviner because these gifts pass from father to sons we are told. But I went to school quite young and by the time I was 12 years old, in 1952, I had already left the village because the school in our village was only up to Standard One. However, the period of over two years of my boyhood during which 1 accompanied my father and watched him performing, left a deep and indelible impression on me.

Whenever we arrived at a village during one of our tours, people who had problems would come round to consult. Charges were high if the situation was grave, but the ordinary charge for common complaints was usually a fowl and the equivalent of 50 FCFA in today's money, about 6.5 pence in pound sterling. When we exhausted the customers in one village, we then moved to another.

There was a variety of complaints. Some people would come in to say that for some days on end they had not had any sleep. Others would say that whatever money they earned 'did not stay in their hands'. Another would wonder whether the third wife he was about to many was from the right family and whether the marriage would be beneficial and long lasting.

My father used to listen attentively to each client's question or complaint. Then he would pick up the five pieces of the wild garden egg, shake them in his hand, spit into the hand containing the pieces, touch the forehead of the client and then throw the pieces to the ground, repeating some phrases which the client had spoken. In case of serious illness in which witchcraft was suspected, the client brought anything that the victim used, for example a piece of his clothing, and this would be put on the floor near the area where the *kaa* was to be tossed.

Then my father, who was called Papa Samba Mburi (he died in 1961), acting as mediator between the client and the *kaa* and the metaphysical world, used his mystical powers to interpret what message *kaa* bad for the client. The dialogue between Papa Samba and the mystical power (*kaa*) and between Papa Samba and the client, and all activities and actions involved would run somewhat like this:

Papa Samba (to the client)

Tell us, what is it that you want us to do for you?

Ta Jato Mankin (the client pointing to the *kaa* and making his request sincerely) Mbuoda. is seriously sick. She is dying and we want to know who has caused it.

Papa Samba (Picks up the five pieces, shakes them, touches the pieces of cloth from the victim, spits on the *kaa*, touches the ground with his hand and tosses them on the floor). They want to know who has caused Mbunda's illness. Who has caused her that illness? Tell me.

Kaa's answer (Interpretation by Papa Samba from the way the pieces fall, and recounting of the message to the client as he deciphers it from the *kaa*)

The cause is within your family circle. It is from a near relative.

Ta Jato Mankiri – (requesting earnestly)

The family member, is he/she from the father or mother's side? Mbunda is seriously sick. She is dying and we want to know who has caused it.

Papa Samba (picks up the five pieces, shakes them, touches the pieces of cloth from the victim, spits on the kaa'. touches the ground with his band and tosses them on the floor). They want to know who had caused Mbunda's illness. Who has caused her that illness? Tell me!

Kaa's answer (interpretation by Papa Samba from the way the pieces fall recounting to the client as Papa Samba deciphers it from *kaa*,

-The cause is within your family circle. It is from a near relative.

Ta Jato Mankiri – (requesting earnestly again)

The family member, is he/she from the father or mother's side?

Papa Samba (picks up the pieces and tosses them to the ground)

They ask if he/she is from the father or mother's side?

Kaa's answer (interpretation by *Papa Samba*)

From the mother's side. She is a woman, an aunt to the victim.

Ta Jato Mankiri (pleased and surprised, smiling and shaking his head).

Is she aunt Biende of Moh Village?

Papa Samba (picks up the pieces and repeats the name suggested by the client while tossing the pieces onto the ground)

Shaking his head – it is a sign of wonder. He is amazed at what he is being told.

Kaa's answer (*Papa Samba interpreting*)

NO! She is innocent. Biende is innocent.

Ta Jato Manari (shaking his head)

Is it Shamo, the aunt from Njema'?

31

Papa Samba (Picks up pieces, repeats the name and place and throws them to the ground)

Kaa's answer (answer not conclusive, some elements in the answer from the way the pieces lay engender doubts)

Papa Samba (repeats the action, calling the name several times and tossing the pieces to the ground a second time)

Kaa's answer (interpretation by *Papa Samba*)

Is she a widow: this lady whose name you called?

Ta Jato Manari (answering firmly)

Yes, her husband died several years ago and she had many children and is not living well.

Papa Samba (repeating action to be sure, throws pieces, picks up the stem, looks at it and leaves it carefully where it was, shakes his head).

Kaa's answer (interpretation by *Papa Samba*)

She is the one. Yes, she is! Kaa says it is she.

Ta. Jato Mankirt (They exclaim: Eeii, Eeii; wemei, wemei, wemei!) What should we do then? It's getting too late. Will she die?

Papa Samba (Picks up the pieces, spits on them in his hand, touches the pieces of cloth of the victim and throws them on the ground repeating what the client said).

It is late. Will she die?

Kaa's answer (interpretation by *Papa Samba*)

You are not late. Go immediately to your home. Take along a *nggogu'* (one of your daughters in your compound who has recently returned from her marital home), catch a white fowl, take a blanket and some mimbo and give them to aunt Shamo.

Before you leave touch the patient with the blanket and with the fowl. When you arrive, tell her this child has 'fallen her', i.e., falls at her feet to ask for forgiveness. If she accepts, the victim will be loosened from where she has been 'tied' because they have been waiting to kill her on the anniversary of Yinda's death.

Ta Jato Manlari and others (Wemei, wemei, wemeii) Papa Samba (instructing the client boastfully)

"If you go and do all that you have been told and there is no change 'then it is not me, Samba Mburi, speaking then I did not inherit this from my forefathers and they will have to resurrect to come and tell the family the truth of which I am now custodian. This we did not buy – you will come back to tell me how it all went. Do not consult me again if I am found to have told you an untruth. Make haste!"

Very often many different people came with complaints and my father would deal with them one after the other and with the same confidence and certainty. Although no one evaluated the success of his art in terms of how many cases came out as predicted, the fact that more and more people came to him each time was evidence enough that he was a successful diviner.

In the past, people in Binshua and other neighbouring villages who wanted to seek revenge for some wrong done against them would go to consult Ta Mbe of Kumanji a quarter in Binshua. He was a famous lightning and thunder-sender, *nwe-tur-mbeng*. He could send lightning and thunder to strike a particular person if he/she was guilty of a crime he had been accused of. If someone's property was stolen or a man ran away with another man's wife. Ta Mbe was capable of' wiping them from the face of the earth', said one admirer of this diviner whom I questioned.

The diviner would set up a raffia palm stem in the ground, at the base of which he laid an axe near a bowl of water. This axe was heated until it glowed; and when he lifted it and dropped it into the bowl of water the steam and the noise was believed to set oft' a flash of thunder and lightning which was directed with a broomstick to the area where the criminals were. It was expected to strike them dead. Ta Mbe still lives today, and although quite old now he still performs his magic and I do not know who in his family will inherit this art. I am told that the reason for this is competition between relations to possess it.

Very often the judgment of lightning and thunder – (*sa'-mbeng*) – first destroys things in the compound of the suspect to signal a warning, and if this is not heeded it is sent again, and then it kills. In consulting a thunder and lightning-sender, one has to be sure of one's facts because lightning, as mentioned earlier, has been reported to return and kill the supplicant. Once it is sent it must either destroy something or rebound upon the sender.

When I was writing this section of the paper, Dr. Michael Rowlands of the University of London and myself visited a famous diviner in the outskirts of Bamenda. We met the diviner, and he was happy to receive us. The evening turned out to be a very stormy one with frightening flashes of lightning and thunder, almost as if by design. Each time it struck and the sky was littered with flashes of lightning and the thunder grumbled the diviner would clasp his fingers several times. Then he told us firmly: 'Do not fear. I catch and send lightning ... so it cannot do you harm here'. We were all very alarmed although he gave us assurances and he wasn't really concerned. Dr. Michael Rowlands will bear witness to the strange events of that day.

In Binshua Village as well as in many other villages of the Mbum group, people consult *ngaa-tur-mheng*, that is, people who control rain. These *ngaa-tur-mbeng*, or rain doctors as they

34

are called, use a mixture of herbs either to cause rain to fall or to stop it from falling. When an important occasion is to come up in the rainy season the people concerned go with the offering of a fowl, a calabash of raffia palm wine and some money to consult a rain doctor. If he accepts the offering then he will 'hold' the rain until the occasion is over. Sometimes two rain doctors are opposing or rivalling each other, one to hold the rain and the other one to make it fall, and then the one who is attempting to hold it will tell you 'the rain is too heavy in my hands' (Mburu John, 17, 1988) and the rain will fall.

I have witnessed the activities of rain doctors many times in the past. On many occasions in the 'fifties when we were to harvest corn in August, at the height of the rains, my father would ask a famous rain doctor in the neighbouring village of Njema' to hold back the rains. That day the sun would shine all day long, and just when we had finished, the sky would open and the rain would pour down heavily for about four hours. Because of this fact many people in the village used to wait and do their harvesting on the same day as we did.

There was an incident in 1953 which has remained indelible in my mind till today. Four of us from Binshua were attending school in Nkor, in Bui Division, very far away from Binshua, because we bad passed to a higher class (Standard Three) which Binshua did not offer. We used to come on some weekends to take provisions back to school.

One Sunday, after a visit home, we were returning to school. By one o'clock when we were to leave, the sky was totally covered with thick nimbus clouds – a sign that heavy rain was expected. We could not delay our departure if we were to trek the nearly 30 miles and arrive by evening so as to be in school on Monday morning. Someone advised us to go to Ta Mbe of Kumanji, the man referred to earlier, who could send lightning and thunder. When we got to his house and told him our plight, he went behind his house to his sanctuary and returned with a wet tuft of grass in his hands. He gave the grass to Frederick Njeke, the eldest among us, and instructed him to travel behind us, and each time it appeared that the rain was catching up with us, to face the rain and blow on the grass towards the direction from which the rain was coming.

We thanked him and with our luggage on our heads, we quickly descended the Mati Cliff to Tabenken, climbed the Mfingong hills and in less than three hours we were overlooking Laan, with Frederick Njeke still behind us holding finnly on to the grass that Ta Mbe had given us. Rain was falling very heavily behind us. Towards evening on the last lap of six miles to Nkor, we passed Laan, and Njeke threw away the grass, unknowingly perhaps. When we were about two miles away from Laan a terrible rain-storm caught up with us. It was so severe that we could hardly move. We tried to pray together like the good and sincere Catholic children that we were, but it was difficult to find the words. We were battered this way and that by wind and hail stones and we could neither return to Laan nor continue to Nkor. Then it got dark and since the wind-buffeted grass had completely covered up the path, we did not know where to go. We grouped our way to within two miles of Nkor only to discover that the River Kibanya had flooded the entire valley to such an extent that we could not go near the valley, not to speak of looking for the hanging bridge which normally spanned the river. In absolute desperation we had to find our way back to Laan pushing the grass aside to find our way. We bad in our confusion lost: our luggage and we got to Laanin complete darkness. There we stayed the night with a very kind woman who was sorry for us, but the night was full of nightmares. We left for school early in the morning to tell the frightening story to the pupils and the teachers. When we went to Binshua some weeks after, Ta Mbe only said that our mistake was that we threw away the grass. Had we held fast to it, the rain would have fallen only after we had passed. May be this was a coincidence? I could not tell then at 13, and even today that I am 47, I still feel unsure!

The Medicine-men (*ngaa-mchep*) of Binshua and the Wimbum area

In Binshua Village in particular and in the Wimbum area generally, the different varieties of performers, described in the preceding section, who range from people said to eat others alive mysteriously (*tfu yingwe*) to kaa' diviners and rain doctors *(ngaa-tur-mbeng)*, are all called witches because they have in common the characteristic of having 'four eyes'. Perhaps this loose nomenclature is understandable in view of the fact that in Wimbum everyone is said to be born with the potential for witchcraft in him, although not everyone is a practicing witch. The distinction thus lies between *nwe-tfu* and *nwe-gee-tfu* that is between a person with witchcraft potential and a practicing witch or wizard. This distinction also explains the fact that in Wimbum cosmology people's witchcraft is rated in degree; therefore the greater the degree of each person's brand and type, the more dangerous he would be.

We have already said that whenever there is a plague, sickness, death or some catastrophe, the Chief and his elders as well as the persons afflicted ascertain the cause through the many avenues available in this land, and take the appropriate steps. The Chief might intervene by a plea and by the offering of a libation to his ancestors, or he might perform a neglected ritual. There is also the drastic step of pronouncing exile; in the past, the accused person could even be executed!

Although some diviners look for the cause of an illness and also prescribe the cure by mystical means, there are also other people who specialize in the cure of illnesses, using for this their knowledge of herbs. The use of these 'native' medicines, as they are called for want of a better terminology, is very widespread. Usually the native medicine-men accompany the curing process with some rituals. Among the many fakes and charlatans there are some medicine-men renowned for their success in treating epilepsy, madness, complicated fractures and a variety of other ailments believed to be caused by witchcraft.

There are many medicine-men in Binshua – in fact it is not too great a claim to make to say that the head of every family and! or compound usually has a number of drugs he uses, some ground and kept in powder form while others are in the form of leaves which are harvested fresh from the bush or from the comer of the house when needed. Illnesses such as headaches and all internal problems are treated in this way. A powder may be administered or a pasty mixture made with red palm oil. Today, as in earlier days, whenever such medicines are licked it is important for the patient to rub his stomach, face or legs, whichever part is affected, with the remnants on his palm. In order to treat internal diseases with ingestible traditional medicines, the practice requires that the traditional doctor first of all tastes his concoction in the presence of his client prior to giving the patient his dose.

Usually the medicines are put into calabashes, traditional bags, bottles and cans, and there is the problem in that the storage of the medicines is not hygienic. The lack of standardization of the dose is also a major problem.

There are some traditional medicine-men who act by removing from the patient's body mysterious objects believed to cause the disease. The medicine-man passes medicines in a container over the body. When he comes to the place where the illness is, the object is removed magically and shown to the victim. Sometimes it is some hair tied up in a small bundle or a stone or a needle. We call such a medicine-man, *nwe-mcho'*, a man able to remove something from your body.

We also have the *nwe-nggang*, who is also able to 'loosen' a victim who has been tied or bound by witches. Very often the witches are said to detain a victim or something of his, such as a piece of cloth or hair, and if a nwe-mcho' can find all these then the patient would be well. He uses his 'four eyes' to do these feats.

Among the Wimbum people, if one loses a valuable thing or does not have a child of his marriage, his maternal uncles, who are always concerned about the children of their sister, would come to *chep-we*, that is, they come along with a *nwe-mkaa*, a ritual priest who will scrape powder from a substance and mark his forehead with it, thus strengthening him so that no one is capable of harming him. The process is called *kwaa-mkaa* and is accompanied by a ritual.

If someone has been initiated or lured into witchcraft, he can be relieved of his witchcraft power by medicine-men who practice *sisi-mmir*, that is the art of nullifying witchcraft power by using medicines to 'blacken the eyes'. Children who are lured into witchcraft are usually treated in this way. My cousin's son, Tantoh, presently studying for his Advanced

Level GCE, was a victim of initiation into witchcraft. The story he tells of how witches bothered him is a long one. It took my uncle, who is still alive, much time and money to save him. Tantoh can tell you stories that leave you in no doubt as to his belief in what some of us might find incredible.

Throughout the Wimbum area the sasswood ordeal *(nnor-nggur)* is used to prove innocence of witchcraft. It was quite common in earlier days but seems to be dying out gradually. If an unexpected death or calamity occurs, the relatives of the victim may offer to undergo the ordeal so as to clear themselves from suspicion of having caused the event. They go to the bush with a skilled sasswood man who administers the sasswood. Sometimes the eldest in the family will drink on behalf of the family. Sometimes, if the case is serious, a whole village may undergo the ordeal. The Wimbum believe that only a guilty person can die from drinking the poison: the innocent vomit it, and So go unscathed. If someone fails to vomit, he may confess his guilt, and then he is saved by the sasswood expert tickling his throat with a feather to make him vomit out the medicine. If someone representing a family vomits after having drunk the sasswood (*nnor-nggur*) then his family is not guilty and the rest need not undergo the ordeal. People who die in the sasswood ordeal are not booed in the compound. Because they are regarded as guilty they are buried in the bush and there is no mourning. There are many sasswood experts in the Mbembe area, in Yamba and Mambila country who are consulted when serious matters arise in the Mbum country.

Another type of ordeal very closely similar to the sasswood ordeal is called *su'si-bsii*, washing the face. Suspected persons wash their faces in the mixture themselves and those who are guilty are affected immediately and some have been said to go blind. A 65-year-old Mbum lady who is recovering from six years of sickness predicted by a *njoo'* diviner, and referred to earlier, told me that she has attempted all these sasswood and 'washing the face' ordeals because her house has been much bothered by witchcraft. About the *su'si-bsii* ordeal she recounted that the medicine-man usually sits alone in a room into which people coming for the ordeal file in one by one to drink or wash their faces. If they are innocent they simply leave the room. However, 'if a witch comes in', she explained, 'although he is shown the pot of mixture he wanders about the room without seeing it'. Then the medicine man splashes the mixture into the eyes and he cries aloud and everyone outside knows what has happened inside. There is bewilderment and satisfaction expressed in shouts and cries, and people peer into the room to see who has been 'caught'.

There are many types of ordeals which come into use and eventually lose favour. There is one in which white cowries are used. The medicine-man points the cowry shell at your eye and if you are innocent it falls to the ground, but if you are guilty it will automatically enter your eye and cause a sharp pain which will provoke a scream. Julie Nketi in Ngarum suffered such a fate for stealing, and since then she has not been able to see properly, so my informant told me.

In Nkanchi not long ago a new ordeal was adopted. A man there has a stone on which people who want to prove their innocence come to sit .The man places a small chicken on the suspected person's head. If he is guilty the chicken flees and some insect, a wasp or a bee, stings him dead there and then! Nothing happens to an innocent person. I was informed that the compound of Pastor Bebe in Nkanchi is nearly empty since most family members died from this ordeal in Mchaar village (Nkanchi) 'because of the stone'. Hundreds of people came from all over the country and beyond to justify themselves. The fame of this medicine-man has been declining recently, however.

There was another case in my own village, Binshua. Of a famous native medicine-man called 'Dr' Yo'mbo' who, at the peak of his power, was consulted by more than a hundred patients a day. He specialized in exorcizing people who were bewitched, and also practiced in the "blackening" or "sealing" of the eyes of people who were initiated into witchcraft. The people of Jit, and this is a recent story, will never forget him, because he apparently uncovered a big pot buried deep in the ground in which people were alleged to have been 'held' mysteriously. When the pot was dug out of the ground it was found to contain such items as shoes, strands of hair, bones and special stones, papers, pens, pencils and parts of vehicles. It was later explained that the presence of the part of a vehicle signified that the villager whose motor-part was found there was to have a ghastly accident and die. This story came into the open when some clients consulted Dr. Yo'mbo' and he insisted that the boy informing them had told the truth of something important he knew. When the presence of his buried pot was reported Dr Yo'mbo' is said to have mounted a search party and dug out this pot 'caught' the people concerned after which many of them left voluntarily on exile to other lands. I was also informed that some of the accused persons committed suicide and others ran away. Some of the Jit suspects are still around and I have made arrangements to interview them. At the height of his power, Dr Yo'mbo' was accused of committing a homosexual act with a Binshua boy called Ngrishi. This crime is uncommon in the area and is regarded as an abomination. Therefore Dr Yo'mbo's fame began to wane and fewer and fewer people consulted him, it being believed that this act destroyed his magical powers.

The most recent case of supernatural powers concerns someone in Nyen village, in Momo Division, who is curing people with water from a spring above his compound. We watched him cure some blind people. Hundreds of people from far and near visit this diviner-healer.

As far as traditional medicine and divination are concerned, it is common for someone to gain fame rapidly only to lose his power soon afterwards. At home we say that the gods were in disagreement because he went against one of the laws of his supernatural gifts.

2

The Witness of Other People

In this section I am presenting other people's viewpoints on the belief in witchcraft practices in Binshua and in other villages in Donga Mantung Division. The aim here is to show that this belief affects the life and fabric of that society so profoundly that only very few people have stood up against decisions to exile them or have refused to go into exile. In fact, it is an instance of someone standing up against a decision to exile him that gave that impetus to conceive this section.

The Witness of Gallus Nchanji

Gallus Nchanji is presently 35 years old, married with seven children. His three years of secondary education took place in St. Augustine's college, Nso', in Bui Division, because during his time there were no post-primary institutions anywhere in Donga Mantung Division, a Division of more than 170.000 inhabitants as at that time. Only the children of parents who could afford the transport and fees went outside the Division to study, and there were very few of them because money was hard to come by in those days. By 1963 only about seven people could boast of a post-primary education in Binshua Village. Ganus Nchanji left school halfway through because of the expense: his father was a catechist working with the Catholic Mission, receiving only 1.000 FCFA monthly for his wages – insufficient even for food for his large family. The father of Gallus Ncbanji knew that a place was reserved in heaven for him, and he had learned and was teaching others that the soul was more important than material and earthly things. So Gallus Nchanji and his brother and sisters grew up in these humble, circumstances many of them ending their schooling after graduating from the one Catholic primary school, the only one in the village.

Gallus had a step-brother who completed and passed his primary school course, obtaining the First School Leaving Certificate. With this qualification he got a job as messenger for the Senior Divisional Officer in Nkambe. Herny Ngala was a very charming, handsome, hard-working and reliable young man, and was very much liked by his boss and by the other workers in this Divisional Headquarters. The many thousands of people whose problems had to be treated by the Senior Divisional Officer passed through Henry to see his boss, and Henry always treated everyone with respect and with sincerity. By this his fame grew.

I had then just been transferred to teach at the Government

Bilingual College, Molyko - Buea, and I went there leaving my family behind in Bamenda. One weekend Dr Yembe, Dr Nwana and myself travelled to Bamenda. I was going to visit my family, as I did from time to time. Sometime after midnight on the Friday night I was woken up by the sound of a bell, and when I got up I was informed that someone called Henry Ngala from our village had died in Buea after I left. When I explained that there was no village boy of that name in Buea that I knew of: the news-bearer, himself from Binshua Village, but doing business in Victoria, informed me that Henry had gone to Buea only that day and died there. He had passed an examination to do a course for Prison Warders in Buea, and when he and his colleagues arrived, as was customary, the entire group was led on a jog up the Buea Mountain towards the Catholic Mission Church in Buea Town. Henry collapsed on the way, arid before attempts could be made to resuscitate him, he had died. The news-bearer told me he had come to give the news so that we could leave for home to arrange for the burial, planned to take place in Binshua that Saturday before mid-day. There was no time to lose, and so I informed my wife, put on my clothes and set out for Binshua Village, which we reached just before dawn. Fortunately for us the Villagers had already learnt of the death through a radio announcement, a common means of communicating such news Cameroon. The usual mourning that takes places had already begun, although there were still people who insisted that the news could not be true. We arrived to confirm that, sadly, it was so.

We lost no time. There was the grave to be dug and we also had to act quickly in order to prepare to entertain the visitors, particularly those from Buea who would accompany the corpse, and those from Henry's former office, including his boss, who bad only returned from a tour that day.

When the corpse arrived it was taken in a convoy to the Divisional Headquarters, and the Senior Divisional Officer and the entire administrative corps led the coffin in convoy to Binshua Village, which is about four kilometres from the office. The young man was buried in grand style in spite of his relatively low grade in the Public Service.

Before the actual interment, Henry's corpse was laid in state in his step-mother's house for his step-father, the SDO, and a few others to see. Because no measures had been taken to preserve it, it had swollen and forced open the coffin, and it was awful and terribly frightening to look at. I saw the startled stepfather step back when he saw the swollen corpse and the few of us who saw it agreed that it should quickly be covered and taken to the grave. Knowing how my people interpret such things, I knew that we were in for difficulties: according to our tradition, a swollen corpse was not a good sign.

However, the burial ceremonies which we carefully planned were carried on successfully, with speeches from friends, representatives from various groups, from the Administration and from the family.

What impressed me very much was the candour of the Senior Divisional Officer in his speech. After expressing his profound sorrow to the family on behalf of the Government and himself, he told the congregation that had he not been away he would have dissuaded the young man from going for that course because, during a recruitment test right there in Nkambe the late

Henry Ngala had collapsed while running and was saved only by the timely intervention of a medical doctor who happened to have been around. This was about the third time that Henry had suffered from this problem and medical autopsy from Buea had stated that he had a cardiac problem. He was going into these details, he said, because he knew what the Binshua people would say after he had left. He stated categorically that nobody should say that witchcraft was the cause of the late Ngala's death, and Promised that the law would descend heavily on any person who promoted among the Population the awful tendency to attribute all sad events to witchcraft. He ended by saying that the late Henry Ngala was a young man loved by himself particularly, and by everyone who came in contact with him, a man of love, sincerity and kindness, and that the family should recover from their tragic loss quickly, without any rancour or witch-hunting.

I was particularly impressed with this eulogy because the Senior Divisional Officer took our hints seriously. We hoped that that warning would do the village some good. But as will be seen later many things do not work as they are designed to.

As soon as the Senior Divisional Officer, his entourage and the guests had left after the entertainment, the rest of the people gathered in the mourning houses, the women to their own and the men to their own, as is the Wimbum custom. They had hardly settled in these *ndap-rkwi* ('houses of death' or mourning houses) when there was a stir, and you could see people running away from the roads leading to the palace. Very shortly after there was confusion and panic and people who were still standing outside dashed for cover. ·A terrifying masked juju, a very dangerous one, had left the Chief's palace and was on its way to *ndap-rkwi*, or mourning house. When someone gave me the hint, I knew that what we feared would take place was in fact doing so.

I do not know when or why I went to the *ndap-rkwi* of the women, but suddenly I saw that the people around the yard there had all vanished and the *chu mbu* (forerunner of the *nwerong* society with a net face-covering) and the *nwerong* delegation with a number of btanta (titled men of the *nwerong* society) came in *chu mbu's* wake to the yard, all looking serious. We knew that there was a very important message for the people; and everyone was anxiously waiting to hear from the senior *tanto'* of the group what the message consisted of

There was an indication, by the solemn waving of hands, that everyone was invited to listen to the important message from the palace. In a matter of minutes a crowd appeared in the yard as large as there had been at the graveside. Then the announcement came:

"All the people of Binshua, listen. *Nwerong* has asked me to inform you that it had been found out that the death of Henry Ngala was the work of a few people who do not want peace and tranquillity in this village; to take away a son in cold blood in broad daylight is a terribly grievous and an unforgivable crime warranting maximum punishment.

Thus *nwerong* had decided as follows: that Ma Yu'bu and Ma Ntala should be given the bamboo. That Gallus Nchanji should be given the bamboo. Let them go, and give us peace. Oh Binshua, this is the message that nwerong has brought to you."

The speaker ended abruptly.

As soon as he had finished and the bamboos were given to those named, the party left immediately back to the palace. Those who were outside did not know what happened to the two women who were in the women's mourning house. One of the accused women, the mother of the deceased, when she heard her name, stood up and missed the way to the door and was instead heading for the window when I caught her and tried to calm her down, but whatever I was saying, nobody had the time to listen. I was so utterly shocked that I thought of driving to Binju to report to the administrative authorities who had warned against what had finally happened. Many people, including the man with whom I had come, persuaded me that apart from the fact that it would amount to fighting a losing battle, it might lead to the Chief being arrested, which would not go down at all well for me in the village. The car we' came in was not mine. Maybe if I had had my own car with me then, I might helve reported the matter. Since then I have never really forgiven myself for that inertia.

As I indicated somewhere in this section, the late Henry Ngala was a step-brother to Gallus Nchanji. Gallus Nchanji was not at home when this thing happened. He had gone to Nigeria to eke out a living for his family and was going to learn of his sentence of exile only through a message sent by some relative. It would mean, of course, a permanent separation from his family.

Six months after this death I went home and everything had settled. To my surprise I saw Gallus Nchanji. The first day I felt somehow reluctant, or rather ashamed, to ask him a question about the terrible exile sentence. When I met him again, or rather when he visited me, I made bold to ask him:

'Tell me Gallus, did you hear the thing that happened here some months ago about you?'

'Do you mean the exile sentence and the accusation that I slaughtered my step brother?' he asked, looking very relaxed!

'Yes, precisely it. I was wondering whether someone gave the message to you in Nigeria', I persisted.

'Yes, of course. Such news travels with the speed of sound; be added humorously.

'Since I returned from Nigeria, it is two months now, no one has spoken to me about it. I was wondering whether the strength of my own witchcraft knowledge is more than that of all the witches of the four quarters of Binshua put together! I am still holding on to see the first person who will ask me, and I am sure the two of us will wear me pair of trousers', he concluded, with a determination that surprised and pleased me a great deal.

We both laughed and discussed in detail the ridiculous assumptions some people make mainly as a result of ignorance and poverty. Two years later, Gallus Nchanji, who is a very prolific writer, wrote an article to be published in the

Cameroon Official Newspaper, 'The Cameroon Tribune' entitled *Why This Superstition?* from which I quote.

... 'RECOURSE *to divination and allied superstitious belief which is fast becoming the order of the day amongst many countries in Africa has driven people to much frustration and untold hatred*

Victimized by fear and ignorance, many persons have come to believe in witchcraft for a couple of strange and dreadful circumstances which they find difficult to interpret. This widely accepted mal-practice also abounds in nearly every ethnic grouping in Cameroon, for which reason Mgr Paul Verdzekov of the Archdiocese of Bamenda in the North West Province issued a 10 page pastoral letter on Superstition addressed to our Christian and heathen communities during the month of October, 1980, condemning the subject in the light of sacred scriptures:

'The Lord Himself had promised us, "I will not fail you or desert you". (Hebrews 13:5-6)

It is perilous for any community to invest its natural, social and economic resources in unproductive consumption such as fetishism, witchcraft, etc. This is surely an appeal to which not only Christians but also intellectuals should give much leadership in the light against such absurdity in society.

Such beliefs great murder of the first Commandment of God or simply, idolatry. The question is, must we therefore continue in our adulthood to lead our own youngsters to hold tenaciously to the belief that superstition is an Ark of refuge from the storms of life?

Watch out, for 'God Alone Gives Us The Security For Which We Long'.

(+ Paul Verdzekov) (Archbishop of Bamenda)

'MY NECK! MY NECK! An evil spirit has gripped my neck, I cannot breathe', etc., etc. was the cry that rent the air in Ghana street in Nkwen for several days. Many people s sound sleep was disturbed by the shouts. And many Africans believe very sincerely that witches and

wizards exist. But who is a witch or wizard? According to African Culture he or she is one whom people allege. by irrational instincts. to be the author of certain calamities such as death, sickness or famine. The accused is generally believed to possess a peculiar demon of distinctive adversity, whereby he or she could injure fellow beings in calculable mysterious ways.

Thus when rioting students mobbed a female colleague to unconsciousness at P.S.S. Batibo in Bamenda recently they contended, rightly or wrongly, that the girl was a witch. What was her offence? She was alleged to have sparked off an unprecedented mysterious disease in the college campus for which 49 victims were hospitalized

ELSEWHERE, in Donga-Mantung, where ritualistic banishment reigned supreme as a deterrent for any bewildering death, a traditional authority ousted the grandson on the allegation that the follow slew his step brother. So swarming in the average African mind is the superstition of witchcraft that whenever misfortune trespasses its course, people literally reiterate the sinister word of witchcraft "ad infinitum". The idea of witchcraft as you probably know is not limited to one set of peoples, but it is distributed through many different cultures, races, and environments. The Western World today peers with condescension on communities which believe in witches; hence Joan of Arc was doomed for witchcraft practice at the time when witches were still being set ablaze in Europe until the dawn of the French Revolution.

As I begin to ponder over this intricate subject, common sense suggests the first question how it happens that ideas so absurd, fantastic and often horrible have been so widely diffused in place and time? One thing is pellucid, given that – the witchcraft idea must be related to something real in human experience; nevertheless, it is not a physical substance.

The witchcraft belief and its concomitant persecution must therefore be a response to psychological strains. Witches work from envy, malice or spite against individuals, rather than in the pursuit of material gain. For instance, amongst the Yamba tribe, no person would dispute that witches turn into birds at night before they go to attend their congresses.

But why have people believed in witches for so long? The reason is that people are in search of a path to relieve their feelings of unease and anxiety. Many people assume that it is very unnatural to die unless one attains an old age! The younger wife who cannot bear children because of a blocked fallopian tube may not know this. Instead she looks for rational causes within her capabilities. 'Why must the senior wife be having children almost every year? If only this old lady could release me, I would also bring forth children. The elder wife thus necessarily becomes a witch as far as the junior concubine and her sympathizers are concerned?

SOMEONE I knew very well had three children and they all died one after another. He came to me, convinced that he had been bewitched 'Why me alone? Why not someone else? Three children in a row! Unnatural! Suspicious! And I'll tell you that it:' my mother-in-law! She is a witch! '. Thus it could clearly be seen that witchcraft is the scape-goat that is responsible for the sufferings that people cannot or will not explain otherwise, and providing a pattern of action that the sufferer may follow when his misfortune keeps him particularly anxious.

THUS if you have cultivated your fields in the usual trend, you may blame a witch for the failure of your crops and so escape from the thought that accepted farming techniques might be at fault. If your illness fails to respond to medical treatment, you may as well blame a witch and so be saved from doubting the worth of medical expertise, etc.

Beware! All witchcraft is a force in social relations that can shatter friendship, ruin a happy marriage, or society. It is a banner under which people are jealous, hateful, denouncing and may even murder one another under unjustifiable pretexts. In psychological terms, the witchcraft psychosis is a state which conditions people to convert their latent animosities into an actionable revenge – in retaliation to an imaginary offence believed to have been committed against themselves by the suspected witch or wizards.

54

OBVIOUSLY there are certain things which defy logical analysis and to which one must confess one's ignorance. African traditional healing is indeed authentic but the witchcraft idea which is entirely non-human phenomenon representing a reverse of moral standard has been unnecessarily patronized by native practitioners because of its obvious attraction of material opulence.

Do you attest to witches? Have you actually seen one? I don't mean persons who confess to being witches. Have you ever attended a witches' conference? Why not drop a note to us.

From the desk of NCHANJI GALLUS
(Journalist/EDUCATOR, CIVIC PATRIOT)
Binshua Village - Nkambe
Donga Mantung
15/06/80.

The Witness of Frederick Ngala Njeke

Mr. Frederick Ngala Njeke was born in Binshua about 50 years ago, into a family which was rich by local standards, because his father had a lot of cattle. As is characteristic in such families in the area, Frederick learnt to work as hard as his father, and he struggled to build up his own independent fortune, knowing that in a polygamous family, as his was, inheritance is a very difficult, sensitive and complex question, the more so in a village like Binshua, in which witchcraft practices find fertile ground in many family feuds.

Frederick is married with nine children from two wives. The first wife, who bore him two children, died in 1967 after a brief illness. Frederick is a very devoted Catholic and uses some of his money to help the Church and the school. He is Chairman of the church committee and with his drive many projects have been accomplished in the Church. He had

55

gripped my attention with accounts of the many incidents he has had to undergo in this village and the shame and humiliation he has suffered there. He states categorically that if he were of little faith he would have left the village on forced or self-exile. Let him speak for himself:

'If I was not a strong believer in God, I would have left his village a long time ago because of the massive campaign of lies and insidious propaganda ... against me. At one point I almost contemplated leaving to find a home out of Binshua.; then, on deep reflection. I thought this will be defeatist and childish on my part since I am a free born son of Binshua. I decided to stay as a challenge.

I know that many of my problems have arisen because of my hard work. Since most of the villagers are lazy, they are jealous and envious of anyone who is bard-working and therefore making progress.

They want everyone to be poor and they usually make pejorative statements like: "You see, Mr. Frederick, although he has many herds of cattle he cannot eat the meat from any of his cows nor can he even drink beer with money from the sales of his cattle. He has joined Nyongo". They want me to sit in the bar all day and dish out drinks then everyone will cheer me up. Can you imagine that when I bought a vehicle it was usually announced to the population that nobody should accept a lift from me and that nobody should be found in the vehicle with me. The people were told that I bad joined *Kupe*·' also. I was not worried by all that smear campaign and blackmail. I knew that, with time, "the truth shall prevail".

In the first few months, whenever I drove past, the Binsbua people would escape into the bush and others actually took cover. In fact most Binsbua people were very attentive to the sounds of vehicles so as to escape from my own in order to avoid being killed, because I would take them to *Kupe* to buy more money, they were told.

Some of my relatives were almost convinced by the propaganda but others went with me everywhere and nothing seemed to happen as bad been foretold. Gradually and gradually some bold people when returning late from the market would join me and arrive home early without any incident. Then at night some people would invite me secretly to carry a woman in labour to Nkambe hospital four kilometres away and I would do that without complaining and without charging any fee. Very soon people started to ask me for lifts during the day and then I began to carry corn from the farms for others and even the Chief himself would come to me for lifts to the extent that when he wanted to celebrate the death of the Fon of Ndu. I was hired to carry all the important Fais of Binshua to Ndu and back. This was at the height of the rainy season and the roads were awfully bad but we returned safely. When I accepted to go, all I said in my prayers was, God if we have an accident on this trip the power of the devil would have succeeded". The LORD did not fail me and we returned safely in spite of the terrible road.

I have had several humiliations in this village. At one point it was announced that nobody should visit me or join a groups in which I am a member. The land I have bad, where my cattle used to be —I transferred them to a new site — has been the source and site of fierce battles between my family and contenders opposed to me. On two such occasions many people were wounded and police intervention was immediate because I had a vehicle and rushed to report the matter, otherwise many people would have died. We have a multiplicity of court and police cases which take a lot of time and effort – all these because of the ill-will towards me.

When my first wife died it was said that I gave her to *Kupe* or to *Nyongo* to get more money. I have wondered and have been baffled by what ignorance can do to a people. I have asked to know this... if it is true that I can give my wife to get rich everyone in the palace should be a millionaire because almost all the reasonable people there are dead and dozens of others have been exiled for practicing witchcraft. Why then is there so much poverty there?

However, I have been so tenacious in this fight because I am a Christian with a forgiving heart. I know that it takes a long time to do away with superstition, particularly in an illite.ra1e society. Slowly and slowly we will succeed in changing the hearts of some people with time. We have joined the crusade of the Cross of Jesus and there is no turning back. Now that you have decided to put these facts in writing my fight is not in vain. You should count on me. Thank you for your good work.

The Witness of Two Churchmen in Binshua: Emmanuel Njiko and Thomas Yinkfu

Accusations of practicing witchcraft made against two important Binshua people would have been contested by many villagers were it not for the consideration that, by doing so, the villagers would have been challenging the long standing traditional beliefs of the people. Both the people accused were formerly catechists of the Binshua Village Church. Both of them can read and write.

One of these, Mr. Emmanuel Njiko, is the father of Gallus Nchanji the first of our witnesses. Mr. Njiko served as catechist in Binshua for over 35 years, bringing up many children of the village to know and serve God. For all his meritorious work over this long period many people in the village praise him highly.

The second is Mr. Thomas Yinkfu, popularly nicknamed 'Chicha Kerr', an ingenious practical man and the town-planner of the Binshua, with a modem outlook.

Let they themselves tell us why, after such long and meritorious services they could be accused of witchcraft practices. They are interviewed by a non-believer in witchcraft.

Interviewer:

Tell me Mr. Njiko, what is it that I hear about witchcraft and the Mission here?

Well, massa, I do not understand. Rumour started circulating in Binshua here that the place of the big pear tree (pointing to the position where a huge avocado pear tree once stood at the entrance to the church compound from Mula Quarter) has in it baskets of dry human meat which, when it is given to children, they are bound to repay with a human person for the witches and wizards to "kill" and "eat". When the tree was cut down we thought all was over but no, we were wrong because it was now given out that we were practicing *Nyongo* in church and that I was luring young children into witchcraft and forcing them to take human meat. This was very embarrassing to me.

Interviewer: Do you believe that witchcraft exists?

Mr. Njiko: You see, I am a Christian and I cannot believe in God and in the devil at the same time. Witchcraft is the work of the devil. I cannot serve two masters, God and Satan. So to me, it does not exist.

Interviewer: Why must such rumours circulate about the Church? We have never heard of this before and it is said that

59

there is no smoke without fire. How can you explain the genesis of this?

Mr. Njiko: I do know that those who circulate these rumours are idle people who are jealous of others. Things like these operate in situations where there is competition, as in this case; where another group is struggling to begin a church in the village they discredit me and by that they win converts. Have you heard them mention the Reverend Father? No, they cannot because the story will be unbelievable; so they find people of their own level. How would you believe that for more than 35 years I have taught children and only in my old age do I become a wizard and lure children to give them human meat so that they give their relatives? However, I know that this is a characteristic of a primitive pagan society. We are not far from that level, I think.

Interviewer: What of you, Papa Thomas Yinkfu? We all know your contribution to this village. How comes it that the villagers are accusing you of all sorts of crimes connected with witchcraft practices?

Papa Yinkfu: Yes, I have been accused of all sorts of crimes like waylaying children who are going to the stream and trying to induce or introduce them into witchcraft by giving them human meat. Some children have actually come up to beat me with fowls. They allege that I am demanding them to pay a debt with people. Some people have wondered why my forest of cuca1yptus tress is doing well and theirs are not. They believe it is magic and some have said that I am taking people to *Nyongo*. All I know is that God is with me and certainly some people here want to use this as a ploy to divert my attention from my work. I do not hate anybody for carrying out such vile propaganda – I only urge them to go ahead, for their payoff will not come from me.

Interviewer: I am told that you were one of the early Christians who did so much to help your people and tried hard to civilise them. Have you fallen out of grace today?

Mr. Yinkfu: We were the first Catholic Christians in this area and I have done my best for this village. Do you see all the streets criss-crossing Binshua village? All were surveyed by me. The road network in Binshua was the best in the entire area and was it not for the greed, jealousy; envy and ill-will that this village is now saddled with, Binshua would be a show case, as it was in the past. Today people have planted coffee right to the centre of what used to be large streets; today dirt and filth cover every area and almost everyone degenerates and thinks only of the easiest phrase to destabilize the society – witchcraft. Only ignorant and lazy people find repose in such words. All those who perpetuate this witch craft syndrome/hysteria will soon find that they can't deceive all the people all the time and it will be their turn to be blamed. There is a time for everything.

Interviewer: What advice have you both to give the people of Binshua who are really suffering from witchcraft hysteria?

Mr. Njiko: As a Christian, remain a good Christian, and practice your faith with without fear or favour. Make more mends than you make enemies and do not be deterred when enemies try to ridicule you. Pray for them and with time the same people will come to apologize to you. I have seen this thrice before.

Mr. Yinkfu: Have a forgiving heart and love all your enemies. Believe in what you are doing and do not be taken up by the fear syndrome and be a good example in community endeavours. Talk only when it is necessary. I have found this to be my soothing balm and saving grace in times of trial.

The Case of a Former Politician

Mr. X is one of the first generation politicians in the Southern Cameroons. Given his career I shall leave him in anonymity. He was a very active politician in the heyday of the period in which Southern Cameroons was ruled as part of Nigeria, and he remained in politics when Southern Cameroons became a state, and even after the Plebiscite when we became the West Cameroon State reunified in a Federation with French-speaking Cameroon. Mr. X headed various Ministerial Departments.

With the integration of West Cameroon into the Unitary State, many of the old guards lost their positions and Mr. X was one of them. After attempting business unsuccessfully, he reverted to his one-time profession – the teaching field. This is where his problems began.

He was appointed headmaster of the Government School in his own large village. When its Chief died in 1982 there was great rivalry for the throne between the princes. It was alleged so goes the gossip – that Mr. X vied for this seat as he, too, was eligible to be a successor. However, some members of the succession council did not like him and therefore tried hard to disqualify him, by accusing him of having greed as a weakness. Mr. X fought back hard and is alleged by his detractors to have deterred likely candidates by telling them that they would die if they ascended the throne. This tactic backfired, it is alleged, because the succession council resolved that they would not have him at all on account of it. Finally a successor was got – a young university graduate –

and this ended all the infighting and rivalry for the much sought-after throne of this dynamic chiefdom.

Mr. X reverted to his work as headmaster and with the broad experience he had gathered over the years, the school became a model. Suddenly, however, and no one can say how it all began, a rumour started circulating that some teachers were practicing witchcraft in the Government School. The rumour travelled so far and wide that attempts to stop it failed. Most teachers and pupils of the school knew that the rumour pointed to their Headmaster, but he himself was unaware of it, and nobody even hinted to him what was being said.

One Monday morning, after a long weekend, the pupils assembled, prayed and disappeared into their classes to learn. The Headmaster, whose arrival in school that day had been delayed by other state duties, then reached the compound. Suddenly, as if an electric charge had touched the children, there was a terrible commotion. Both teachers and children fled in all directions for cover, the smaller children leaping through the windows. In a few minutes the entire compound was deserted!

After two days Radio Bamenda reported this deplorable incident as a news items. The radio station ended by appealing to teachers and pupils to return to school. It took a number of days for the school to resume fully and the Headmaster was transferred to duties in educational administration. Nobody ever investigated this extraordinary affair.

Mr. X has retired since then and he now lives in his native village. Many people there continue to conduct an insidious campaign of slander against which he has no ready remedy. It appears that there is a coordinated attempt to make life difficult for him. I have heard some people recalling unlucky accidents in his life, some of which took place many decades ago, to suggest that these had a mysterious significance. Some have said that when he was a Minister he bought a tractor which rolled down the road in Buea and crashed in a gully, killing its driver. Others say that on another occasion the belt of his com mill killed its operator. These accidents, which have been elaborated in the telling, are now said to point to his having been involved in witchcraft for many years, and it is even suggested that there is something eerie and dubious about the businesses he is running now. All this, said about someone in a traditional society, am ac1ually bring into contempt and demean the individual concerned. Why so much should be said about a man who seems so harmless is a matter that someone should take time to unravel. What is the motive? One characteristic of our society, alas, is that people believe in things which are absolutely ridiculous, especially, as has been pointed out, when there is competition for high office or when a man rises above his fellowmen by his/her own efforts.

The Witness of Paul N. Langdji

Mr. Paul Ngong. as he was popularly known in those days, opened the primary school which is in Binshua today, in the early 40s. He was transferred and later on returned there in 1957 as headmaster. In fact this writer taught under him as a pupil teacher in 1957 and benefited very much from Mr. Paul's shrewdness as a leader and from the competence and alertness of an inspiring boss.

After many transfers in his long career Paul settled to teaching among his own people in the village of Nkor in the

Noni area in Bui Division. In this village, stories started circulating that Paul was planning to give school children in for *Kupe*, that in actual fact he had buried a pot in the school in which children's finger nails were rut and stored and that the eventual outcome would be that one day, when lightning struck, it would destroy a large number of school children all at once; some said fifty would die! As these stories developed the village population began to get more and more anxious and disturbed. It is not certain what the last straw was but we are told that the Parent Teacher's Association (PTA) of the school organized a secret meeting at which they resolved that Paul was practicing witchcraft and that he Senior Divisional Officer (SDO) should be asked to transfer him. The PTA copied to Paul the letter they had written to the Senior Divisional Officer. Paul replied demanding that they prove their baseless allegations.

Instead of waiting to get a reply from the SDO whom they had petitioned, the group came to school and drove him away from the class and then began to plan to kill Paul by attacking his entire household. The headmaster of the school was forewarned of the plans being made to take the life of this member of his staff so he sneaked in, in time to warn Paul and his children. They narrowly escaped capture, he escaping by the back door. The story of this dramatic escape is told in many versions in Nkor today, some even saying that Paul disappeared in a transformed state!

If this plan had succeeded it would have shown how a few people can scheme and manipulate a group to create problems which could have far-reaching consequences.

We are told that Paul did not take this lying down. In the following days the forces of law and order descended on Nkor and eight people were arrested and detained in Kumbo, the divisional capital. We were informed that the case was actually taken to the magistrate's court. The case was tried and the Suspects were discharged and acquitted on technical grounds, because it was argued that women were among the men but were not also arrested.

It is revealing to note that Paul stood as candidate in the parliamentary elections of April 1988 and the results from the Noni area show a lot of support for him in spite of the feelings of some Noni people about the case. This indeed was a very encouraging sign. In our last interview with some Noni people in July 1989 it was remarked that the population of Nkor has now realized that there was actually no truth in the matter. The Nkor people have now come to realize that there was a clique behind the entire drama and are now friendly with Paul with whom they not only drink together but also exchange visits.

The fact that Paul Langdji succeeded in standing for the parliamentary elections as a candidate for this area allows the story to be seen in its correct perspective and reveals the intrigues of some interested parties, who thought that they could challenge his candidature in this way.

The Witness of Thomas Kimbi

The reader who is yet unconvinced by my testimony and by the declarations of these other people so far discussed, will hopefully be impressed by the example of a school teacher who has had more than his fair share of blame in the many areas in which he has taught.

Thomas Kimbi was born in a polygamous family in Tabenken fifty-two years ago. He is married and has nine children.

The accusation Thomas faced in 1987 was that he 'ate' his own cousin. His cousin, Mr. Francis Yi.mwe, himself a grade two teacher, died one day when returning from the Jah Village weekly market. He had bought some vegetables (huckleberries) and on descending the stiff cliff to Tabenken, he fell over the edge down the cliff and died as a result. Later that evening the wife raised an alarm because the husband, who did not usually come home late was unusually late that day. A search was conducted all night to find him, to no avail. In the morning he was discovered down in the Kurbarr COO: already dead. It was the traces of huckleberries which he had bought in the market and which had dropped from his bag which gave the despairing searchers the due that finally led them to discover that he had slipped down this dangerous cliff. Other Tabenken informants prefer to say that he was lying by the corner of the road, not down the cliff and that, in fact, he was hidden from the view of passers-by by witchcraft art!

The news of this death was shattering to the villagers and devastating when it reached the village Chief

As usual, the diviners were set to work to find the cause of this death, an 'unnatural' one according to the family members. The suspects were of course Thomas Kimbi and his brother Peter Ayaba. Not only were they accused directly of the crime of 'eating' their cousin, Peter Ayaba was actually assaulted by the Chu Mbu' (a messenger member of the secret society in a net face-covering) who lashed him in public. In anger Peter actually retaliated by beating the Chu Mbu', an unforgivable, unforgettable and unheard of crime in the tradition of the Mbum people. He then escaped and took refuge in the Catholic Mission from the onslaught of the traditional authority. This was a very sensible thing for Peter to do if he was to escape death. In the end the village Chief, who himself is a devoted Catholic Christian, was eventually convinced by the combined efforts of the priests not to give Peter Ayaba a bamboo, to forgive Peter for beating the Chu Mbu' and thus to ignore the witchcraft charge. It was this intervention that has allowed Thomas and Peter to remain in Tabenken till today.

I am also reliably informed that Peter was then asked to *lep nggong* (appease the earth/world) that is, to pay a sort of fine of 'six things' to atone for this sacrilege committed so that this ransom is distributed to the six quarters of Tabenken according to the customary formulas. It is said that he publicly refused to conform and that people do not know what to do next. However, all the people there say that there is no one who is above the will of the people and that there is no sheer force in witchcraft practices.

Meanwhile Thomas, Peter and the entire family members have been banned from visiting people in the village and vice versa. They have been ostracized by Tabenken society; while they still live there it can be very embarrassing indeed. Recently, however, people have begun to visit them. In filet, on my last visit to interview Thomas there was a friend visiting him and after a three-hour interview many more friends joined us for a while.

Divinations continued for some time after the death of Mr. Francis Yunwe. It later emerged from the said divinations that neither Thomas nor Peter was to be held responsible for the death of their cousin. In fact, when the family consulted a *nkieng* diviner, the relatives found that none of the accused persons bad appeared in the bowl of water when the supposed culprits were invoked. Instead it was 'his own body' (wife) whose image came into the water! The relations were now caught in an awkward situation and were faced with the awful choice of either destroying 'his own body' and causing more hardship, or allowing that evil one to go on living with people. The way things have gone so far shows that they decided on the latter course for obvious reasons. One of my informants gave me this information which was confirmed by Mr. Thomas himself.

It is difficult to apportion blame for a false accusation to any of the persons involved in this witchcraft episode because of the way the events have unfolded. What is still not clear to me or to anyone reading this story is who Mr. Thomas Kimbi actually is and what it is about him that creates so many problems for him as he moves from place to place. Mr. Thomas Kimbi is a qualified grade two teacher and has a charming personality, He has taught in twenty-one different schools since he began teaching in 1957, beginning as a pupil teacher in Binju and rising to his present level. The record of Mr. Thomas Kimbi's career presented below is alarming and demonstrates the treatment a dutiful servant can receive at the hands of an overbearing employer.

The main accusations concerning Thomas are that he distributes human meat to school children and later on requests them to repay the debt with their relatives. It is said that he also 'eats' people and the example quoted are his relatives, one being Mr. Ngeh Fidelis, who was burnt in his mother's house, and the other Mr. Francis Yimwe, the cousin on account of whom Thomas was first accused and finally divined as innocent.

In many villages where Thomas taught many people have many things to say about this witchcraft scenario and they tell many tales about him. For example, one story goes that in Upper Mbot Thomas is said to have hung human meat in a tree. Then the tree dried up. The seers of the village discovered this and one morning a dangerous *ngwerong* (an executioner masked hooded with raffia cloth) came out to capture him and, 1o, he transformed and mysteriously fled! Others say that in Lower Mbot Thomas and a certain Chrysanthus Ngha brought human meat to the school to distribute to the children. The children reported this to their parents and a *nggiri* group (a secret cult of the Princes) and *Shey Nggiri* (leader of the cult) came out to warn those practicing witchcraft in the school to stop it because they had been 'seen'. At the end of the year the people asked that he be transferred.

In Tabenken it was alleged that Thomas was selling human meat and that he kept it at the back of a pickup 404 vehicle belonging to Mr. Mburu, a businessman. The people with 'four eyes' who defend the village asked the Reverend Father to remove him from the school or else they would not send their children to the Catholic School.

I have learnt, only recently, after a long investigation of this case, that Thomas has possibly been the target of slander by a relative of his. It is being suggested that there was a family disagreement about the safekeeping of some bride wealth and that one family member had sworn that his heart would only be at rest if Thomas was sacked from his work. It is thought that this relative was behind the accusation and had gone to most villages at which Thomas has taught to poison the minds of the people against Thomas so that he should become unpopular and thus be sacked. Is it possible that this relative would have travelled to the more than 20 locations, some of them very remote and some very far off where Thomas has taught?

70

Whatever the truth of the matter is, this case is an illustration of the unjustified mental torture and physical humiliations that many people are subjected to in some of these rural areas in which the witchcraft phenomenon prevails.

Death Sentence for Murder of Mother, and Wife
A vicious murderer who killed his mother and wife is to face the firing squad.

The Kumbo High Court last December 15 sentenced Daouda Nyuze to firing squad for killing his mother and wife. While summing up the case Mr. Justice Ambe Moutchia described the offence as heinous and that the accused deserved no mercy from the state. He said the evidence of the prosecution proved Mr. Daouda Nyuze actually killed his mother, Biy Adama, and Mairama Shahla, in normal state of mind. Mr. Justice Moutchia wondered how a patient of "waist pain, minor malaria and liver problems" could commit murder. He said that Daouda Nyuze's claim of being given to witchcraft by his relations was not enough for him to kill. The judge noted that even medical reports were not enough to testify whether the accused was insane. According to him the law provides room for the judiciary to "decide the question of insanity through its own observation".

The prosecution further presented five witnesses and seven exhibits before the judge.

Facts

The facts of the case are that the accused had stabbed the mother and wife for allegedly giving him to witchcraft. Mr.

Daouda Nyuze was admitted in a traditional healing home belonging to Damasius Tatah at Kitiwum in Bui Division for waist pain, malaria and liver problems. He was there until November 6 and was now capable of splitting firewood and fetching water. On the fateful day, he left for his home in Takui, some two and half kilometres from the healing centre. While returning Daouda Nyuze is said to have attacked a passer-by with a knife. When he arrived, Kitiwum after midnight, he stabbed his mother and his nursing wife who were all asleep. The accused gave himself up to the gendarmerie and admitted he also wanted to eliminate his brother. He claimed that these people had given him to witchcraft.

Before judgment was passed, Daouda Nyuze pleaded for leniency saying he had three children who will suffer in his absence. The judge ignored his plea and sentenced him to firing squad.

Peter Adi Fonte
(CAMNEWS)
Cameroon Tribune Tuesday, January 30, 1990, No. 989
pg 4.

3

Witchcraft and the Law

In many of the modem African states of today, there is only sketchy legislation relating to witchcraft. For instance, in the Republic, of Cameroon and in the Federal Republic of Nigeria, the legislation is limited to a single section in the Penal Code (in the case of Cameroon) or Criminal Code (in the case of Nigeria), the section simply providing a penalty for acts of witchcraft. There is no attempt to define the term witchcraft. One may conjecture that the reason for the absence of comprehensive legislation concerning witchcraft may be that witchcraft has no overt physical characteristic and as a result, it cannot be proved by either documentary or oral evidence as can ordinary offences such as stealing, assault, forgery, murder, and so on.

The absence of these physical elements in the offence of witchcraft irresponsible for the fact that in the traditional African environment divination and trial by ordeal were, and still are, commonly resorted to as a means of identifying witches. The penalty for witchcraft in pre-colonial times might be more severe than today's customary punishment of exile from the community: torture was once common and the most notorious offenders were either burnt or otherwise executed, to rid the community of them and to deter others from following their example.

There is no gainsaying the filet that every civilized country in the world today had passed through this rather primitive period of witchery with its attendant trails by ordeal, confessions extracted by torture, and cruel executions, and has evolved to a civilization' with modern types of offences and comprehensive laws designed to combat them.

It is unfortunate for African communities that their own patterns of development from earlier times have not been based on their own intrinsic communal values. When the colonial powers partitioned Africa among themselves they interrupted and drastically influenced these patterns of development with foreign notions. The British colonialists did not hesitate to abolish some of the African native laws and customs simply because they were alien to their own culture of that era, although their professed ground were that the practices were 'repugnant to natural justice, equity, and good 'conscience'. An example of the latter was the condemnation of trails by ordeal, made illegal in 1903. The French, in their own African colonies, emasculated African laws and customs through their policy of assimilation. Although some may feel that this colonial attitude towards African native laws and customs served its purpose at that particular time, it was an interference which blocked and distorted an empirical evolution of a legal history and jurisprudence of our own, better suited to our own societies. To argue that we have blamed Europe enough for this misfortune dodges the issue. Europe can never be blamed sufficiently for her part in preventing Africa's natural self-development.

The colonialists transported metropolitan laws to the African colonies and set up courts presided over by expatriate magistrates and judges (in all but domestic and minor criminal matters). These courts disregarded divination and based their judgments only on material evidence, documentary testimony, oral evidence or medical evidence. Since, by its very nature, witchcraft could not be proved in this way, it was not recognized as an offence *per se* by the colonial legal system.

There was, however, insufficient manpower to staff the colonial administration and judiciary to anything like contemporary standards. Apart from the doctrine of colonial self-sufficiency in finance, there were demands for the services of well-educated Europeans at home and service in the colonies was not attractive by comparison. The British were compelled by lack of manpower as well as for ideological reasons (for they respected tradition to some degree) to introduce the system of Indirect Rule in most of their African colonies. This was particularly so in Nigeria, where the people were ruled as far as it was possible through the instrumentality of the local Chiefs, and their councils, in accordance with the guidelines of Lugard, the Governor-General at the time of the end of German rule in Cameroon.

The colonial administrators did not therefore have many direct dealings with the people but dealt with them largely through the Chiefs, and mainly through interpreters. The system of Indirect Rule enabled some of the practices of witchcraft and divination, among other native practices, to survive among the people, to the full knowledge of the local Chiefs but concealed from the colonial administrators, whose dealings with the indigenous people were limited, as we have seen. This explains why, despite the ambivalent attitude of the British colonialists towards witchcraft, and in particular towards witch-finding ordeals, it remained so widespread and deep-rooted among local people right up to independence.

With independence, instead of the African states enacting comprehensive legislation on witchcraft, they have been busy enacting laws in line with the inherited colonial laws, contenting themselves with including a single section in their respective Codes punishing 'acts of witchcraft'. In the Republic of Cameroon witchcraft is punishable under Section 251 of the Penal Code which stipulates:

Section 251- Witchcraft

Whoever commits any act of witchcraft, magic or divination liable to disturb public order or tranquillity, or to harm another, in his person, property or substance, whether by taking of a reward or otherwise, shall be punished with imprisonment for from 2-10 years and with a fine from 5.000 to 100.000 francs. (Emphasis mine)

I have no doubt that many Francophone African states have broadly similar provisions in their respective penal laws; the African *evolue* has usually retained some vestiges of the metropolitan practices and laws which he has been taught to admire. And in the Federal Republic of Nigeria, witchcraft is punishable under Section 210 of the Nigerian Criminal Code which ordains as follows:

'Offences in relation to witchcraft and juju' 210: Any person who –

a) by his statements or actions represents himself to be a witch or to have the power of witchcraft, or

b) accuses or threatens to accuse any person with being a witch or with having the power of witchcraft, or

c) is guilty of a misdemeanour and is liable to imprisonment for two years (Emphasis mine)

Many Anglophone African states which inherited the British Colonial Laws at independence, such as Ghana and Uganda, have provisions differing little from that of Nigeria, quoted above. The Nigerian Criminal Code echoes something of the old English offence of 'Pretended Witchcraft'.

Notice that nowhere in the two representative sections of the Penal Laws which are reproduced here above, is the word witchcraft defined by the draftsmen. With due respect to the draftsmen, the two sections are rather vague, and the Cameroon section is unfortunately further plagued by ambiguity. As far as the Anglophone provinces of Cameroon are concerned, decisions on cases involving witchcraft generally circumvent their witchcraft aspects.

It is most regrettable that so many decades after independence we should still show such downright naivety, and luke-warmness towards witchcraft, a matter which affects almost all of us. Isn't it unfortunate that for all this length of time, we would appear not to have any positive legislative plans as to how to cope with this social reality, belief in witchcraft, which perpetually endangers the very existence of most of our people?

Some people opine that an explanation for the fact that our approach to legislation on matters such as witchcraft, divination and magic, is so evasive or passive lies in a desire to imitate the developed countries in order to earn the respect of the United Nations and the allied institutions thereof. The argument is that if we do not tailor the legislation of our states on the pattern of the laws of the so-called civilized nations, the United Nations or any other international organization could say of us, 'since the laws of that country cannot be equated with those of Europeans or North Americans or with those of Eastern Bloc countries, the

77

country can only be regarded as primitive and cannot expect our approval and our aid'. Therefore, in order to become a member of the community of nation, we must 1ishion our state legislations on the pattern of the laws of the so-called civilized nations, regardless of the filet that they do not reflect the social realities of our own country.

In spite of all, it is imperative for us to know what lies behind the phenomenon of witchcraft, the source of its mystery and fascination, how it functions, and why people believe in it, because it is not sufficient for us to simply dismiss its existence as fanciful in public while back home, in our respective villages, we are face to face with its various manifestations. This is tantamount to double standards and is being unrealistic as modem Africans. Legislation on the matter should not be based on the arbitrary inheritance of colonial Jaws, but should be preceded by thorough investigations and studies of the matter. This done, we can also say that we are at the beginning of our own scientific revolution!

4

Witchcraft and Religion

As has already been stated, in the Wimbum area, as in many African societies, the belief in witchcraft practices is so entrenched in the lives of the people that any attempt to convince the people that the existence of this mysterious power is mere fantasy, is a bootless, futile exercise. In fact, it will not be exaggerating to say that in most of the traditional African societies more than 90 per cent of the people organize their lives around the principle of witchcraft.

It is normal for many Africans to go to church on a Sunday morning and immediately after church, if some serious illness or death bas struck the family, to go to a sorcerer or *'nggambe man'* (diviner) to find out who has caused the problem. Many an African Christian would not see any conflict in practicing aspects of the imported Christian religion as well as offering sacrifices to their ancestors. In so far as they are concerned there is no contradiction in this dual existence, even if in the western world and in the 'civilized' nations there is obviously a contradiction with their beliefs because witchcraft is opposed to science. Science is rational the filets are verifiable and objective, whereas witchcraft is subjective, belief in it being nurtured by poverty, illiteracy and ignorance. Science, long associated with progress in the reduction of hunger and disease, seeks to know the why 'and wherefore of things, while continually testing its own assumptions against new evidence. Witchcraft negates science and in most cases it is anti-progress, being a closed system of explanation. Admittedly, however, organized experimental science is not part of our culture whereas witchcraft practice is.

Someone who turns to the Church when confronted by a grave misfortune is likely to be advised to pray for the courage to accept it as an occasion to participate in the suffering of Christ. There is relatively little emphasis, for example, in the mainstream Christian denominations, on the ministry of healing so characteristic of the public ministry of Christ and the early apostles) and, moreover) no explanation is provided for the occurrence of a misfortune. For most Africans their traditional beliefs provide at least an opportunity to 'know' the cause of a misfortune, even if there is no means of reversing it. For example, if a sudden death occurs, the diviner may attribute it to witchcraft by a member of the family, or to the angering of a dead ancestor by the neglect of a sacrifice or libation. Once the cause is established, measures can be taken which, in the minds of those who believe in them, will prevent similar misfortune in future. Thus, some Psychological relief is provided, if only temporarily, and what is life but a continual coming to terms with psychological trauma?

Many Africans including those highly educated welcomed the Christian message of salvation from the outcome of sin, while being unwilling to forego seeking comfort from a belief in the possibility of avoiding misfortune through traditional means.

Thus a large majority of Africans in their traditional setting are only nominal Christians. To expect true Christianity in the western sense from them would be demanding too much, because in Africa, belief in witchcraft, imbibed from birth, influences the whole outlook on life, whereas this is not generally the case in Europe and the temperate parts of the world to which its peoples migrated in great numbers.

The established religions present different concepts of life and death from those that belong to most traditional African belief systems. A live person, in the Christian sense, is a moral person. He/she has a soul. When a child is born, for example, he/she is not a moral person until he/she is baptized. For the Christian, a human body is the Physical container of the soul. When it dies the body rots and turns to dust, but the soul lives on, going to either heaven or to hell depending on how the human person lived on earth, because he/she had to give an 'account of his/her stewardship'.

The Wimbum concept, and probably that of people in many African societies, is that a human person is made up of a body and a spirit and that death is the process of passing from one life to another.

When a person dies the spirit-double can move out of the body and re-enter this world by getting into the womb of a woman and being born again. That is why in some societies that I know, when some person of importance dies, the women scramble to have sex with anybody they find that night in the hope that they will become the mother of the reincarnated spirit of the notable.

Alternatively, when you die you can join your ancestors who went before you to continue the family in another realm. The ancestors are believed to be waiting to receive the newly dead ones so that they find out how the rest on earth are living. As you arrive, it is said that you would face a barrage of questions from anxious relations – 'How is Mabong, how is Tashey?' etc, they would ask. It is believed that if you were wicked to an ancestor when he/she was alive, or did not celebrate his/her death properly, he/she will make sure you sulfer when you too are dying. You will be punished for not sacrificing to ancestors. This belief is supported by the fact that some people who suffer for a long time in their sick bed die as soon as they confess, or perform a certain libation. It is also believed that if you bewitched any relations or tormented many people, when you die, your ancestral family will reject you and you will go to live on your own. That is why many people build small shrines on the graves where libations, to solicit ancestral support, are poured in time of adversity.

The strict observance and attachment to the ancestral cult is absolutely fundamental to African life. A contradiction arises for most acculturated Africans and they develop a dual personality, because they are taught to accept an additional set of assumptions. As Fr Kofon states, when talking about the Catechist of Lolo and his acceptance of the New Religion: 'the catechists are trained by the missions to play hide and seek with their own beliefs'.

'They themselves have been successful in their learning of the missionary teaching only by accepting an additional set of assumptions. There is no evidence that they replace their earlier ones.' (p. 146.)

It is thus not surprising, then, that caught in this problem of self-discovery, and self-actualization and confused at the same time by the perplexing forces of nature which sometimes provoke them beyond human endurance, many Africans are very ambivalent about their belief.

Some people argue that people in the African traditional societies are wont to slide so easily towards evil or towards the devil including witchcraft, because, as downtrodden peasants existing in an environment where evils such as high infant mortality, malnutrition, poverty, disease and witchcraft prevail, they have more hope in the devil than in the true God, believing that God has abandoned them.

If the argument seems banal and puerile, it is only because we fail to appreciate the magnitude of the problems facing them; problems which seem to offer them no glimmer of hope for the future, problems ranging from abject poverty among them and discrimination against them, to various forms and guises 'of exploitation by those whom, according to them, God seems to favour. Still, some people contend that if the Church were to truly recognize the anxieties of the victims of calamities caused by witchcraft practices, perhaps it would pave the way for more profound studies into this mysterious power which many Africans are believed to possess and which they use mainly for evil ends,

Other people, however, think that even in the advanced societies, a witchcraft mentality of a dangerous type persists. They have argued that as witchcraft cycles seem to correspond with certain periods of rapid change in the evolutionary processes of human civilization, we are today at the stage where Europe was in the sixteenth-seventeenth century, with its terrible and spectacular witch trials, described by some writers as the 'age of the witch craze'. If so, even if it might take us very long indeed, we may well also arrive one day at a stage where fear and suspicion of that terrible-something about-to-happen and/or the fear of a confrontation with a monstrous enemy whom we see in our dreams, will lead us, too, to build-up an incredibly elaborate system of defences in the hope of protecting 'our people'. Whatever you like to call this mentality – call it power bloc politics, ideological differences, cold war, even political witch-hunting or spy-mania the end results are the same. If you kill with a 'mystical power' and I kill with a 'civilized weapon' both end up in the loss of human life, although we are usually made to understand that one way is somehow holier than the other. 'Our' notoriety in these matters can always be explained away, as many national governments do today, in terms of the logic of defence. After all is not logic' our' preserve, the preserve of the civilized world?

The Christian Church in Africa is caught in this delicate and dramatic task of releasing millions of its Christians from the nightmare of this all-pervading belief in witchcraft. The Church does not however teach that witchcraft does not exist and has never done do, because in the New Testament there are incidents in Our Lord's life which could be interpreted as His treating demoniac or satanic possession, for example, the incidents involving the Gadarene swine (Mt. 8:28-35; Lk. 8:26-39; Mk. 5:1-20) the dumb demoniac (Mt. 9:32-34), the epileptic demoniac (Mt.17:14-20). Even in the Old Testament, references to this art abound; see Exod. 22: 18. Levi. 19:31.20:27; Deut. 18: 10. 2Kings 9:22. 2Chron. 33:6. Isaiah 57:3. Jeremiah 27:9 and 1Samuel. 28:3. 28:7. The Church holds that the devil can do things using human beings and since the concept of the devil as a counterforce to the will of God is upheld and taught, anyone who acts as a servant to the devil or is in league with him offends God. The Church thus condemns such actions from that point of view. The Church does not want us to believe that witchcraft or anything satanic does not exist otherwise Our Lord's triumph over evil would be without foundation.

The Church, however, has a problem because it is difficult to know who is under the influence of the devil. If someone performs unusual feats could he/she not be using other knowledge not from the devil? Where, for example, does the devil come in when a diviner interprets his *kaa'* or his spider and a sorcerer his/her *njoo*?

Most African witchcraft centres around mystical cannibalism, that is, the alleged act of 'eating' people mysteriously, and around the change into various forms for the purpose of destruction. It is very difficult either to prove or disprove claims to such activity because metaphysical systems are not open to proof by scientific methods. Therefore we must conclude that since man does not yet know everything, we should still strive to reduce our ignorance, rather than give up the attempt in frustration.

I do not imply that the Church condones, or in any way approves of devil rites. On the contrary, she wholeheartedly opposes them. In the words of the Reverend Father Chrysanthus Tim:

'she [the Church] knows from experience that human nature is weak, that it suffers from imagination morbid fancy, terror of the unknown, private spite knavery, credulity and hallucination. She does her utmost to fight them with all the weapons at her disposal'.

There have been many writers on the subject of witchcraft in the Christian Church, some as early as the tenth century. Some writers quote the example of Herodiana (the daughter of Herodias in the New Testament of John the Baptist's time) as being possessed by the devil.

A good many cases of accusations of witchcraft in Europe have been recorded such as those against the famous Essex witches, recorded by Macfarlane. The most notable period of witchcraft accusations and trials in Europe was that of the fifteenth, sixteenth and early seventeenth centuries, after which they diminished gradually. The case of St. John of Arc being convicted of being a witch and heretic, and condemned to burning at the stake in the market place at Rouen, in France, in 1431, provides a typical example of the power of the irrational belief in witchcraft and the punishment that it leads to for innocent people. The last English execution of a witch took place in 1684, and the last recorded case of a witch being burnt in Europe was in 1793. Today, in many countries, particularly in the developing world, the practice of witchcraft is still as strong as in the past, although in the Wimbum area in particular and in Cameroon as a whole, modernized indigenous forms, as well as commercial imported varieties, are on the increase, while traditional forms are diminishing. A discussion of some of these follows:

Kupe is a name of a mountain, one of the highest volcanic peaks of the Manenguba range in Mwaneguba Division of the South West Province of Cameroon. *Kupe*, as a form of witchcraft, is a near equivalent of *nje* nchang in Mbum, that is, the other-world of tempting wealth. People are supposed to go there to exchange human beings for wealth. This name gained popularity because of the myths about the mountain among the Bakossi people. Many people in Anglophone Cameroon would refer to someone who has suddenly become rich or someone who has worked hard to make money, as someone who has gone to *Kupe*. Sometimes attempts are made by the society to ostracize such people, as was noted in the witness of Frederick Njebe and 'Mr. X', or even Paul Langdji.

Famla actually means an abandoned compound, the equivalent in Mbum of *Fuurla'* or a ghost town. The meaning of this word in the context of witchcraft is that a witch, having given all his people mysteriously to his/her witch partners to eat (these are usually seven in number) the compound is empty or abandoned. The witch then becomes very wealthy. *Famla* is ascribed to the Bamileke people, a group of very industrious and enterprising people in the Grassfields of Cameroon. One suspects that belief in *Famla*, has gained currency because the Bamileke are considered by many people to be mean and stingy, in spite of their wealth. The word Famla has gained such a mystical force that no one will dare write, investigate or talk about it lest he/she dies. In these days, when someone dies suddenly, it is said that he/she has joined Famla or has been given, sometimes unwittingly.

Nyongo is a form of witchcraft practiced mostly among the Bakweris of the South West Province and the Douala's of the Littoral but the concept has gained currency among many other tribal groups, especially among the Wunbum of Donga Mantung. It is the same idea of giving people to get wealth. Rich people are always accused of having joined *Nyongo*. If someone of yours dies the result is the same. You are suspected of giving him to the witch group – to *Nyongo*.

Kong is a new form of sorcery practiced particularly among the Douala people of the Coastal province, but which has spread (*see Annexe*), It is said that someone 'claims the life of a person who will work in the other world for the benefit of the former, the profits being credited straight to his/her bank account'. Variations of this practice abound among the Creole people of West Africa. We are informed that mostly, when a husband has accumulated some wealth and has built a good house, the wife will give him to be killed and when he is in the next world he helps to build up what was established for the wife on earth. In filet, there is said to be an association of widows in some big towns of the country formed by rich women whose husbands died in mysterious circumstances. The Government had made some pronouncements on this before in an attempt to arrest the situation. The problem, of course, is how to prove that someone was actually killed mysteriously by the wife or that the women joined *Kong!* These modem forms of witchcraft have gained very rapid ground in the last fifteen years, particularly in the towns and in particular villages where there are some cowards who have become enslaved by fear of it.

So the Church does realize that the practice of witchcraft, and belief in it, in all its forms, does exist and abhors it. However, where elements of the pagan culture do not conflict with the gospel, the Church allows them to coexist with her established practices and adapts them to her own purpose, as she has done since the earliest days of her existence. Also, she shows compassion towards those not yet able to break away from pagan practices: for example, the Church has outlawed polygamy throughout the world but sees that it is still being practiced by a large number of people and perhaps realizes that if it were drastically abolished there might be a return to some old practices like slavery or even the slave trade and bondage. Although she does not tolerate it she sympathizes with its victims and insists that they may be one with Christ.

Most of the Christian churches watch all these upheavals and study them carefully – the Church is very slow at taking decisions on controversial issues, but once it is convinced, it goes all out to guide its Christians and stands firmly on its decisions.

Although the Church has no apologies to make regarding some of its stance on the practice of witchcraft, it would be worthwhile and useful to make a more profound study of this mysterious power which people claim to have, and by exposing it, to release millions held in awe of it and thus exposed to the risk of slipping towards the devil unwittingly. It is not only useless but futile to try to disregard the existence of witchcraft beliefs – 'Fantasy or not, belief in the existence of this mysterious power and its exciting uses permeates African societies like the air we breathe, the belief is too deeply rooted to be overlooked.

5

Conclusion

A large part of what you have been reading is my attempt to record my experience as a child in Binshua, some 47 years ago, with the aim of showing how life in the community was permeated throughout by belief in witchcraft.

However, my aim is not simply to provide what is regarded as a historical record, albeit a very personal one, based on reminiscences of childhood, but to show that even today, belief in witchcraft is very widespread, and that it exerts a profound influence on society, not only in Binshua but in other parts of Cameroon also. To show this I have provided accounts of the experience of others, some of them very recent, and have given examples of what injustices and suffering can be caused by the notion that any misfortune must have been caused by witchcraft.

I regard it as very likely that the situation I have described is very similar throughout Africa and indeed in many other parts of the world too. I can say with certainty that there are many people who have a stock of stories and experiences not very different from mine.

A good number of educated Africans, though by no means all, consider the belief in witchcraft as nothing more than primitive superstition born of human fear – they say that the conquest of fear could eliminate the problems caused by this belief. Like them, I feel strongly that the Devil cannot harm anyone unless God allows it. That is why I have not had any reason to equip myself with charms or *layas* against any sort of witch craft, or to get worthless antidotes or anti-witchcraft protection – signs of human uncertainty and the increasing sense of modern social insecurity.

For the people in traditional society, such as is found in the Wimbum area and the greater part of Africa, anything not immediately understandable is witchcraft. Thus witchcraft for them is synonymous with mystery. Many educated Africans, too, revert to traditional attitudes in stressful situations. As you probably will have noticed, I have seldom been prescriptive or judgmental, and there has been a lot of vacillation in my description of the witchcraft phenomenon. This had helped me to sort out my personal convictions about this phenomenon, so awesome and perplexing to anyone who has grown up in an environment where it is so dominating. I am aware of some contradictions the study has raised and I believe these need more research.

It may be thought surprising that in spite of the impact of Christianity, Western culture and the improved level of education, the majority of people still believe in witchcraft, and that this phenomenon not only persists but is increasing. On the other hand, by the time you finish reading this you may find it difficult to say how far the force of witchcraft is real, and how far imaginary.

What this force is, what to do about it and how to survive from its influence should be the concern of everyone. In-depth studies need to be involved, and the combined efforts of all men of goodwill in all comers of the globe.

References

Kofon, E.N. <u>Africa's Top Secret</u>, Ms.pp.146-147.

Chrysanthus, Tim. 'The Christian Church's attitude towards Witchcraft. Answers from a questionnaire, November 1988.

Rowlands Michael and Wamier, J. P. (1988). 'Sorcery, Power and the Modem State in Cameroon', MAN Vo1.23/ J/March 1988,p. 129.

Kofon, E.N. ibid.,p.159.

Other Written Sources Consulted

Byrne, Patrick (1979). Witchcraft in Ireland, The Mercier Press: Cock.

Chilver, E. M. (1963). 'Native Adminis1mtion in West Central Cameroon 1902 – 1954', in Kenneth Robinson and Frederick Madden (eds.) Essays in Imperial Government presented to MaIgay Perbam. Oxford: Basil Blackwell.

Chilver, E. M. (1986). 'Thaumaturgy in Contemporary Traditional Religion: the Nso' Case'. Seminar Paper for Oxford University Theology students.

Douglas, Mary (1970). (ed.) Introduction to Witchcraft Accusations and Confessions, Tavistock Publications: London.

Gebauer, Paul (1964). Spider Divination in the Cameroons, Milwaukee Public

Museum, Publications in Anthropology 10, North American Press: Milwaukee.

Hawkesworth, E. O. (1923). Bamenda Division, Nsungli Assessment Report. Mair, Lucy (1968). Witchcraft, Penguin: Harmondsworth.

Mburu, John (1988). 'Witchcraft Among the Wimbum', Dissertation, Regional Major Seminary, Bambui.

Newton, R. (1935). Bamenda Division, Mbembe and Misaje Intelligence Report. Padderatz, Dr Gerhard F. J. (ed.) (1984). Africa Tell Africans No. I, Vol I, Harare, Zimbabwe, pp. 6 - 8, 16.

Pollock, J. H. H. (1926). Bamenda Division, Mbembe Assessment Report.

Ritzenthaler, Robert and Pat (1962). Cameroons Village, An Ethnography of the Bafut MalikWaukee Public Museum, Publications in Anthropology 8, North American Press: Milwaukee.

Annexe

Reports of Kong and Nyongo in the *CAMEROON TRIBUNE*, 1989

Ntem

Olamze Will Now Expose Its Wizards and Witches

Witchcraft is still the order of the day in the Olamze District. Ntem Division (South Province).

This remark was made by the Chief of District of Olamze when he visited the village of Mekomengona some 1 kilometre from Olamze recently.

The aim of the visit was to investigate witchcraft practices following rampant reports on the frequent deaths alleged to have been caused by wizards and witches who practice '*Kong*'.

'*Kong*' is said to be Olamze's population killer and it has caused the educated elite not to return to the villages after retirement.

Mr. Bitoumou Mbalale, the Chief of the district, invited the population to denounce and expose any persons suspected of belonging to the *Kong* club.

He remarked that most of the villages are empty today and those involved in the practice of witchcraft do not seem to see the damage they have caused to the population.

The chief of the district advised that the best way of fighting against witchcraft is by getting involved in self-help development projects.

He added that most of those who practice witchcraft are unemployed and believe that the best way of occupying themselves is by stopping the others from progressing.

Achanyi-Fontem

Fako

Woman Arraigned For Witchcraft

Judgment will be delivered February 6, 1989, on a witchcraft case at the Muyuka Magistrate Court. Mrs. Nanyongo Ndive Lucy has been standing trial on a charge of attempted murder punishable under section 251 of the Penal Code.

According to the prosecution the accused is alleged to have earmarked her brother, a military officer attached to the military hospital in Buea, for death.

A traditional healer, Janyidang Jacob Mbu Dieman is reported to have *'rescued'* him from a *'medicine pot'* in which he is alleged to have been *'chained'*.

During the crowded court sessions, the prosecution revealed that the military officer had led the traditional healer to his sister's (accused) residence where a number of items were uncovered below her bed. These included a *'Nyongo'* broom, a Guinness bottle, one penny, a mirror, razor blades, a pin, a padlock and other strange items.

Anxious observers are expected to throng the court on February 6, 1989, to listen to what has been described in Muyuka as the case of the year.

Denis Ngalla (for CAMNEWS)